MW01035415

EURIPI[illegible]

ANDROMACHE

HECUBA

THE SUPPLIANT WOMEN

ELECTRA

THE COMPLETE GREEK TRAGEDIES

Edited by David Grene & Richmond Lattimore

THIRD EDITION *Edited by Mark Griffith & Glenn W. Most*

ANDROMACHE *Translated by Deborah Roberts*

HECUBA *Translated by William Arrowsmith*

THE SUPPLIANT WOMEN *Translated by Frank William Jones*

ELECTRA *Translated by Emily Townsend Vermeule*

The University of Chicago Press CHICAGO & LONDON

MARK GRIFFITH is professor of classics and of theater, dance, and performance studies at the University of California, Berkeley.

GLENN W. MOST is professor of ancient Greek at the Scuola Normale Superiore at Pisa and a visiting member of the Committee on Social Thought at the University of Chicago.

DAVID GRENE (1913–2002) taught classics for many years at the University of Chicago.

RICHMOND LATTIMORE (1906–1984), professor of Greek at Bryn Mawr College, was a poet and translator best known for his translations of the Greek classics, especially his versions of the *Iliad* and the *Odyssey*.

The University of Chicago Press, Chicago 60637
The University of Chicago Press, Ltd., London

Printed in the United States of America

22 21 20 19 18 17 16 15 14 13 1 2 3 4 5

ISBN-13: 978-0-226-30877-7 (cloth)
ISBN-13: 978-0-226-30878-4 (paper)
ISBN-13: 978-0-226-30935-4 (e-book)
ISBN-10: 0-226-30877-4 (cloth)
ISBN-10: 0-226-30878-2 (paper)
ISBN-10: 0-226-30935-5 (e-book)

Library of Congress Cataloging-in-Publication Data
Euripides.
[Works. English. 2012]
Euripides. — Third edition.
volumes cm. — (The complete Greek tragedies)
ISBN 978-0-226-30879-1 (v. 1 : cloth : alk. paper) — ISBN 0-226-30879-0 (v. 1 : cloth : alk. paper) — ISBN 978-0-226-30880-7 (v. 1 : pbk. : alk. paper) — ISBN 0-226-30880-4 (v. 1 : pbk. : alk. paper) — ISBN 978-0-226-30934-7 (v. 1 : e-book) — ISBN 0-226-30934-7 (v. 1 : e-book) — ISBN 978-0-226-30877-7 (v. 2 : cloth : alk. paper) — ISBN 0-226-30877-4 (v. 2 : cloth : alk. paper) — ISBN 978-0-226-30878-4 (v. 2 : pbk. : alk. paper) — ISBN-10: 0-226-30878-2 (v. 2 : pbk. : alk. paper) —ISBN 978-0-226-30935-4 (v. 2 : e-book) — ISBN-10: 0-226-30935-5 (v. 2 : e-book) —ISBN 978-0-226-30881-4 (v. 3 : cloth : alk. paper) — ISBN 0-226-30881-2 (v. 3 : cloth : alk. paper) — ISBN 978-0-226-30882-1 (v. 3 : pbk. : alk. paper) — ISBN 0-226-30882-0 (v. 3 : pbk. : alk. paper) — ISBN 978-0-226-30936-1 (v. 3 : e-book) — ISBN 0-226-30936-3 (v. 3 : e-book)
1. Euripides—Translations into English. 2. Mythology, Greek—Drama. I. Lattimore, Richmond Alexander, 1906–1984. II. Taplin, Oliver. III. Griffith, Mark, Ph. D. IV. Grene, David. V. Roberts, Deborah H. VI. Arrowsmith, William, 1924–1992. VII. Jones, Frank William Oliver, 1915– VIII. Vermeule, Emily. IX. Carson, Anne, 1950– X. Willetts, R. F. (Ronald Frederick), 1915–1999. XI. Euripides. Alcestis. English. XII. Title. XIII. Series: Complete Greek tragedies (Unnumbered)
PA3975.A1 2012
882′.01—dc23

2012015831

⊗ This paper meets the requirements of ANSI/NISO Z39.48-1992 (Permanence of Paper).

CONTENTS

Editors' Preface to the Third Edition · vii

Introduction to Euripides · 1

How the Plays Were Originally Staged · 7

ANDROMACHE · 11

HECUBA · 65

THE SUPPLIANT WOMEN · 133

ELECTRA · 187

Textual Notes · 251

Glossary · 259

EDITORS' PREFACE TO THE THIRD EDITION

The first edition of the *Complete Greek Tragedies*, edited by David Grene and Richmond Lattimore, was published by the University of Chicago Press starting in 1953. But the origins of the series go back even further. David Grene had already published his translation of three of the tragedies with the same press in 1942, and some of the other translations that eventually formed part of the Chicago series had appeared even earlier. A second edition of the series, with new translations of several plays and other changes, was published in 1991. For well over six decades, these translations have proved to be extraordinarily popular and resilient, thanks to their combination of accuracy, poetic immediacy, and clarity of presentation. They have guided hundreds of thousands of teachers, students, and other readers toward a reliable understanding of the surviving masterpieces of the three great Athenian tragedians: Aeschylus, Sophocles, and Euripides.

But the world changes, perhaps never more rapidly than in the past half century, and whatever outlasts the day of its appearance must eventually come to terms with circumstances very different from those that prevailed at its inception. During this same period, scholarly understanding of Greek tragedy has undergone significant development, and there have been marked changes not only in the readers to whom this series is addressed, but also in the ways in which these texts are taught and studied in universities. These changes have prompted the University of Chicago Press to perform another, more systematic revision of the translations, and we are honored to have been entrusted with this delicate and important task.

Our aim in this third edition has been to preserve and strengthen as far as possible all those features that have made the Chicago translations successful for such a long time, while at the same time revising the texts carefully and tactfully to bring them up to date and equipping them with various kinds of subsidiary help, so they may continue to serve new generations of readers.

Our revisions have addressed the following issues:

- Wherever possible, we have kept the existing translations. But we have revised them where we found this to be necessary in order to bring them closer to the ancient Greek of the original texts or to replace an English idiom that has by now become antiquated or obscure. At the same time we have done our utmost to respect the original translator's individual style and meter.
- In a few cases, we have decided to substitute entirely new translations for the ones that were published in earlier editions of the series. Euripides' *Medea* has been newly translated by Oliver Taplin, *The Children of Heracles* by Mark Griffith, *Andromache* by Deborah Roberts, and *Iphigenia among the Taurians* by Anne Carson. We have also, in the case of Aeschylus, added translations and brief discussions of the fragments of lost plays that originally belonged to connected tetralogies along with the surviving tragedies, since awareness of these other lost plays is often crucial to the interpretation of the surviving ones. And in the case of Sophocles, we have included a translation of the substantial fragmentary remains of one of his satyr-dramas, *The Trackers* (*Ichneutai*). (See "How the Plays Were Originally Staged" below for explanation of "tetralogy," "satyr-drama," and other terms.)
- We have altered the distribution of the plays among the various volumes in order to reflect the chronological order in which they were written, when this is known or can be estimated with some probability. Thus the *Oresteia* appears now as volume 2 of Aeschylus' tragedies, and the sequence of Euripides' plays has been rearranged.
- We have rewritten the stage directions to make them more consistent throughout, keeping in mind current scholarly under-

standing of how Greek tragedies were staged in the fifth century BCE. In general, we have refrained from extensive stage directions of an interpretive kind, since these are necessarily speculative and modern scholars often disagree greatly about them. The Greek manuscripts themselves contain no stage directions at all.

- We have indicated certain fundamental differences in the meters and modes of delivery of all the verse of these plays. Spoken language (a kind of heightened ordinary speech, usually in the iambic trimeter rhythm) in which the characters of tragedy regularly engage in dialogue and monologue is printed in ordinary Roman font; the sung verse of choral and individual lyric odes (using a large variety of different meters), and the chanted verse recited by the chorus or individual characters (always using the anapestic meter), are rendered in *italics*, with parentheses added where necessary to indicate whether the passage is sung or chanted. In this way, readers will be able to tell at a glance how the playwright intended a given passage to be delivered in the theater, and how these shifting dynamics of poetic register contribute to the overall dramatic effect.
- All the Greek tragedies that survive alternate scenes of action or dialogue, in which individual actors speak all the lines, with formal songs performed by the chorus. Occasionally individual characters sing formal songs too, or they and the chorus may alternate lyrics and spoken verse within the same scene. Most of the formal songs are structured as a series of pairs of stanzas of which the metrical form of the first one ("strophe") is repeated exactly by a second one ("antistrophe"). Thus the metrical structure will be, e.g., strophe A, antistrophe A, strophe B, antistrophe B, with each pair of stanzas consisting of a different sequence of rhythms. Occasionally a short stanza in a different metrical form ("mesode") is inserted in the middle between one strophe and the corresponding antistrophe, and sometimes the end of the whole series is marked with a single stanza in a different metrical form ("epode")—thus, e.g., strophe A, mesode, antistrophe A; or strophe A, antistrophe A, strophe B, antistrophe B, epode. We have indicated these metrical structures by inserting the terms

STROPHE, ANTISTROPHE, MESODE, and EPODE above the first line of the relevant stanzas so that readers can easily recognize the compositional structure of these songs.

- In each play we have indicated by the symbol ° those lines or words for which there are significant uncertainties regarding the transmitted text, and we have explained as simply as possible in textual notes at the end of the volume just what the nature and degree of those uncertainties are. These notes are not at all intended to provide anything like a full scholarly apparatus of textual variants, but instead to make readers aware of places where the text transmitted by the manuscripts may not exactly reflect the poet's own words, or where the interpretation of those words is seriously in doubt.
- For each play we have provided a brief introduction that gives essential information about the first production of the tragedy, the mythical or historical background of its plot, and its reception in antiquity and thereafter.
- For each of the three great tragedians we have provided an introduction to his life and work. It is reproduced at the beginning of each volume containing his tragedies.
- We have also provided at the end of each volume a glossary explaining the names of all persons and geographical features that are mentioned in any of the plays in that volume.

It is our hope that our work will help ensure that these translations continue to delight, to move, to astonish, to disturb, and to instruct many new readers in coming generations.

MARK GRIFFITH, *Berkeley*
GLENN W. MOST, *Florence*

INTRODUCTION TO EURIPIDES

Little is known about the life of Euripides. He was probably born between 485 and 480 BCE on the island of Salamis near Athens. Of the three great writers of Athenian tragedy of the fifth century he was thus the youngest: Aeschylus was older by about forty years, Sophocles by ten or fifteen. Euripides is not reported to have ever engaged significantly in the political or military life of his city, unlike Aeschylus, who fought against the Persians at Marathon, and Sophocles, who was made a general during the Peloponnesian War. In 408 Euripides left Athens to go to the court of King Archelaus of Macedonia in Pella (we do not know exactly why). He died there in 406.

Ancient scholars knew of about ninety plays attributed to Euripides, and he was given permission to participate in the annual tragedy competition at the festival of Dionysus on twenty-two occasions—strong evidence of popular interest in his work. But he was not particularly successful at winning the first prize. Although he began competing in 455 (the year after Aeschylus died), he did not win first place until 441, and during his lifetime he received that award only four times; a fifth victory was bestowed on him posthumously for his trilogy *Iphigenia in Aulis, The Bacchae, Alcmaeon in Corinth* (this last play is lost), produced by one of his sons who was also named Euripides. By contrast, Aeschylus won thirteen victories and Sophocles eighteen. From various references, especially the frequent parodies of Euripides in the comedies of Aristophanes, we can surmise that many members of contemporary Athenian audiences objected to Euripides' tendency to make the characters of tragedy more modern and less heroic, to represent the passions of women, and to reflect recent developments in philosophy and music.

But in the centuries after his death, Euripides went on to become by far the most popular of the Greek tragedians. When the ancient Greeks use the phrase "the poet" without further specification and do not mean by it Homer, they always mean Euripides. Hundreds of fragments from his plays, mostly quite short, are found in quotations by other authors and in anthologies from the period between the third century BCE and the fourth century CE. Many more fragments of his plays have been preserved on papyrus starting in the fourth century BCE than of those by Aeschylus and Sophocles together, and far more scenes of his plays have been associated with images on ancient pottery starting in the same century and on frescoes in Pompeii and elsewhere and Roman sarcophagi some centuries later than is the case for either of his rivals. Some knowledge of his texts spread far and wide through collections of sententious aphorisms and excerpts of speeches and songs drawn from his plays (or invented in his name).

It was above all in the schools that Euripides became the most important author of tragedies: children throughout the Greek-speaking world learned the rules of language and comportment by studying first and foremost Homer and Euripides. But we know that Euripides' plays also continued to be performed in theaters for centuries, and the transmitted texts of some of the more popular ones (e.g., *Medea, Orestes*) seem to bear the traces of modifications by ancient producers and actors. Both in his specific plays and plots and in his general conception of dramatic action and character, Euripides massively influenced later Greek playwrights, not only tragic poets but also comic ones (especially Menander, the most important dramatist of New Comedy, born about a century and a half after Euripides)—and not only Greek ones, but Latin ones as well, such as Accius and Pacuvius, and later Seneca (who went on to exert a deep influence on Renaissance drama).

A more or less complete collection of his plays was made in

Alexandria during the third century BCE. Whereas, out of all the plays of Aeschylus and Sophocles, only seven tragedies each were chosen (no one knows by whom) at some point later in antiquity, probably in the second century CE, to represent their work, Euripides received the distinction of having ten plays selected as canonical: *Alcestis, Andromache, The Bacchae, Hecuba, Hippolytus, Medea, Orestes, The Phoenician Women, Rhesus* (scholars generally think this play was written by someone other than Euripides and was attributed to him in antiquity by mistake), and *The Trojan Women*. Of these ten tragedies, three—*Hecuba, Orestes,* and *The Phoenician Women*—were especially popular in the Middle Ages; they are referred to as the Byzantine triad, after the capital of the eastern Empire, Byzantium, known later as Constantinople and today as Istanbul.

The plays that did not form part of the selection gradually ceased to be copied, and thus most of them eventually were lost to posterity. We would possess only these ten plays and fragments of the others were it not for the lucky chance that a single volume of an ancient complete edition of Euripides' plays, arranged alphabetically, managed to survive into the Middle Ages. Thus we also have another nine tragedies (referred to as the alphabetic plays) whose titles in Greek all begin with the letters *epsilon, êta, iota,* and *kappa*: *Electra, Helen, The Children of Heracles* (*Hêrakleidai*), *Heracles, The Suppliants* (*Hiketides*), *Ion, Iphigenia in Aulis, Iphigenia among the Taurians,* and *The Cyclops* (*Kyklôps*). The Byzantine triad have very full ancient commentaries (scholia) and are transmitted by hundreds of medieval manuscripts; the other seven plays of the canonical selection have much sparser scholia and are transmitted by something more than a dozen manuscripts; the alphabetic plays have no scholia at all and are transmitted only by a single manuscript in rather poor condition and by its copies.

Modern scholars have been able to establish a fairly secure dating for most of Euripides' tragedies thanks to the exact indications provided by ancient scholarship for the first production of some of them and the relative chronology suggested by metrical and other features for the others. Accordingly the five volumes of this third edition have been organized according to the probable chronological sequence:

Volume 1:	*Alcestis*: 438 BCE
	Medea: 431
	The Children of Heracles: ca. 430
	Hippolytus: 428
Volume 2:	*Andromache*: ca. 425
	Hecuba: ca. 424
	The Suppliant Women: ca. 423
	Electra: ca. 420
Volume 3:	*Heracles*: ca. 415
	The Trojan Women: 415
	Iphigenia among the Taurians: ca. 414
	Ion: ca. 413
Volume 4:	*Helen*: 412
	The Phoenician Women: ca. 409
	Orestes: 408
Volume 5:	*The Bacchae*: posthumously after 406
	Iphigenia in Aulis: posthumously after 406
	The Cyclops: date unknown
	Rhesus: probably spurious, from the fourth century BCE

In the Renaissance Euripides remained the most popular of the three tragedians. Directly and by the mediation of Seneca he influenced drama from the sixteenth to the eighteenth century far more than Aeschylus or Sophocles did. But toward the end of the eighteenth century and even more in the course of the nineteenth century, he came increasingly under attack yet again, as already in the fifth century BCE, and for much the same reason, as being decadent, tawdry, irreligious, and inharmonious. He was also criticized for his perceived departures from the ideal of "the tragic" (as exemplified by plays such as Sophocles' *Oedipus the King* and *Antigone*), especially in the "romance" plots of *Alcestis*,

Iphigenia among the Taurians, *Ion*, and *Helen*. It was left to the twentieth century to discover its own somewhat disturbing affinity to his tragic style and worldview. Nowadays among theatrical audiences, scholars, and nonprofessional readers Euripides is once again at least as popular as his two rivals.

HOW THE PLAYS WERE ORIGINALLY STAGED

Nearly all the plays composed by Aeschylus, Sophocles, and Euripides were first performed in the Theater of Dionysus at Athens, as part of the annual festival and competition in drama. This was not only a literary and musical event, but also an important religious and political ceremony for the Athenian community. Each year three tragedians were selected to compete, with each of them presenting four plays per day, a "tetralogy" of three tragedies and one satyr-play. The satyr-play was a type of drama similar to tragedy in being based on heroic myth and employing many of the same stylistic features, but distinguished by having a chorus of half-human, half-horse followers of Dionysus—sileni or satyrs—and by always ending happily. Extant examples of this genre are Euripides' *The Cyclops* (in *Euripides*, vol. 5) and Sophocles' *The Trackers* (partially preserved: in *Sophocles*, vol. 2).

The three competing tragedians were ranked by a panel of citizens functioning as amateur judges, and the winner received an honorific prize. Records of these competitions were maintained, allowing Aristotle and others later to compile lists of the dates when each of Aeschylus', Sophocles', and Euripides' plays were first performed and whether they placed first, second, or third in the competition (unfortunately we no longer possess the complete lists).

The tragedians competed on equal terms: each had at his disposal three actors (only two in Aeschylus' and Euripides' earliest plays) who would often have to switch between roles as each play progressed, plus other nonspeaking actors to play attendants and other subsidiary characters; a chorus of twelve (in Aeschylus' time) or fifteen (for most of the careers of Sophocles and Euripides), who would sing and dance formal songs and whose Chorus Leader would engage in dialogue with the characters or offer comment on the action; and a pipe-player, to accompany the sung portions of the play.

All the performers were men, and the actors and chorus members all wore masks. The association of masks with other Dionysian rituals may have affected their use in the theater; but masks had certain practical advantages as well—for example, making it easy to play female characters and to change quickly between roles. In general, the use of masks also meant that ancient acting techniques must have been rather different from what we are used to seeing in the modern theater. Acting in a mask requires a more frontal and presentational style of performance toward the audience than is usual with unmasked, "realistic" acting; a masked actor must communicate far more by voice and stylized bodily gesture than by facial expression, and the gradual development of a character in the course of a play could hardly be indicated by changes in his or her mask. Unfortunately, however, we know almost nothing about the acting techniques of the Athenian theater. But we do know that the chorus members were all Athenian amateurs, and so were the actors up until the later part of the fifth century, by which point a prize for the best actor had been instituted in the tragic competition, and the art of acting (which of course included solo singing and dancing) was becoming increasingly professionalized.

The tragedian himself not only wrote the words for his play but also composed the music and choreography and directed the productions. It was said that Aeschylus also acted in his plays but that Sophocles chose not to, except early in his career, because his voice was too weak. Euripides is reported to have had a collaborator who specialized in musical composition. The costs for each playwright's production were shared between an individual wealthy citizen, as a kind of "super-tax" requirement, and the city.

The Theater of Dionysus itself during most of the fifth century BCE probably consisted of a large rectangular or trapezoidal dance floor, backed by a one-story wooden building (the *skênê*), with a large central door that opened onto the dance floor. (Some scholars have argued that two doors were used, but the evidence is thin.) Between the *skênê* and the dance floor there may have been a narrow stage on which the characters acted and which communicated easily with the dance floor. For any particular play, the *skênê* might represent a palace, a house, a temple, or a cave, for example; the interior of this "building" was generally invisible to the audience, with all the action staged in front of it. Sophocles is said to have been the first to use painted scenery; this must have been fairly simple and easy to remove, as every play had a different setting. Playwrights did not include stage directions in their texts. Instead, a play's setting was indicated explicitly by the speaking characters.

All the plays were performed in the open air and in daylight. Spectators sat on wooden seats in rows, probably arranged in rectangular blocks along the curving slope of the Acropolis. (The stone semicircular remains of the Theater of Dionysus that are visible today in Athens belong to a later era.) Seating capacity seems to have been four to six thousand—thus a mass audience, but not quite on the scale of the theaters that came to be built during the fourth century BCE and later at Epidaurus, Ephesus, and many other locations all over the Mediterranean.

Alongside the *skênê*, on each side, there were passages through which actors could enter and exit. The acting area included the dance floor, the doorway, and the area immediately in front of the *skênê*. Occasionally an actor appeared on the roof or above it, as if flying. He was actually hanging from a crane (*mêchanê*: hence *deus ex machina*, "a god from the machine"). The *skênê* was also occasionally opened up—the mechanical details are uncertain—in order to show the audience what was concealed within (usually dead bodies). Announcements of entrances and exits, like the setting, were made by the characters. Although the medieval manuscripts of the surviving plays do not provide explicit stage directions, it is usually possible to infer from the words or from the context whether a particular entrance or exit is being made through a door (into the *skênê*) or by one of the side entrances. In later antiquity, there may have been a rule that one side entrance always led to the city center, the other to the countryside or harbor. Whether such a rule was ever observed in the fifth century is uncertain.

ANDROMACHE

Translated by DEBORAH ROBERTS

ANDROMACHE: INTRODUCTION

The Play: Date and Composition

We are not certain when and where Euripides' *Andromache* was first produced. According to an ancient commentary on the tragedy, some scholars in antiquity drew upon the play's apparent anti-Spartan sentiment to date it to shortly after the beginning of the Peloponnesian War (which began in 431 BCE), and they also said that it was not staged in Athens. Metrical evidence suggests it was composed around 425 BCE. Some modern scholars, pointing to the prominent role played by northern Greece, especially Thessaly and Molossia, in this tragedy, have suggested that Euripides intended to appeal to audiences from that area. But no one knows for sure whether or not the play was in fact first produced in Athens, and—if not—why and where it first debuted instead.

Ancient scholars praised various speeches in the play and said it was one of Euripides' "second plays." Whether this means that the play took the second prize in a dramatic competition, or was good but not as good as Euripides' very best plays, or was second-rate in our sense, or indeed whether it means something else altogether, is uncertain.

The Myth

Andromache dramatizes what might have happened in the years after the Greek soldiers returned from the Trojan War. Andromache had been the wife of the great Trojan warrior Hector; one of the most moving episodes of the *Iliad* shows their meeting, together with their baby Astyanax, on the walls of Troy. Now the war is over, Hector has been killed by Achilles, and Troy has been destroyed. Andromache is the slave of Achilles' son Neoptolemus at his home in Thessaly, and she has borne him a child. Neoptolemus has married the wellborn Greek girl Hermione, daughter of Menelaus and Helen, but their marriage has not produced any children. While Neoptolemus is away at Delphi to try to reconcile himself with Apollo, whom he blamed for his father's death, Hermione and her father try to kill Andromache and her son. At the last moment the two are saved by the intervention of Peleus, the father of Achilles and grandfather of Neoptolemus. Then Orestes, the son of Agamemnon and cousin of Hermione, arrives unexpectedly, reporting that he has arranged for Neoptolemus to be killed at Delphi. He takes Hermione away, for she had been promised to him before her marriage to Neoptolemus.

The bloody aftermath of the Trojan War—including the Greeks' murder of Andromache's baby Astyanax and her enslavement by Neoptolemus, the son of the very same man who had killed her husband—was recounted in ancient Greek legend in gruesome detail and was often depicted in ancient Greek art. Euripides himself dramatized these events repeatedly, for example in *Hecuba* (written only a year or two after *Andromache*) and *The Trojan Women* (written about ten years after *Andromache*). So too, the death of Neoptolemus at Delphi was well established in Greek mythology and poetry, though accounts of exactly how and why it happened diverged considerably. By contrast, Hermione was a shadowy character about whom little had been reported in Greek legend other than that she was the daughter of Menelaus and Helen and married Neoptolemus. The sudden appearance of Orestes in this play surprises the other characters and has perplexed some modern readers. But it should be recalled that, as Agamemnon's son, he is not only the cousin of Menelaus' daughter Hermione but also may be playing out, a generation later, his own version of his father's hostility to Achilles that is portrayed so memorably in the *Iliad*. The same mythic material dramatized in the *Andromache* was also the subject matter of some other fifth-century tragedies, including a *Hermione* by Sophocles and plays by Philocles and Theognis. But little is known about the plot of Sophocles' play and almost nothing about the others, and the dates of all of them are unknown.

Transmission and Reception

The troubled destiny of Andromache after the Trojan War fascinated ancient readers and theatrical audiences, perhaps even more in Latin poetry than in Greek. The Latin Republican tragedian Pacuvius wrote a *Hermione* of which only a few fragments survive; Virgil created a memorable episode in his *Aeneid* in which Aeneas meets an aged Andromache now remarried to the Trojan seer Helenus; and Ovid composed a verse epistle in his *Heroides* in which Hermione, abducted by Neoptolemus, writes to Orestes, asking him to save her. How much such later texts are indebted to Sophocles' tragedy *Hermione* or to other lost Greek versions of the story rather than to Euripides' *Andromache* is uncertain.

Euripides' play survived as a text in the schools and for some private readers, and it belongs to the group of his ten plays that were most widely diffused during ancient and medieval times. By contrast, the events Euripides dramatized here have left no trace at all in ancient pictorial art.

In modern times *Andromache* has never been among Euripides' most popular plays, and it has rarely been staged. But it has served as inspiration for a number of highly successful dramatic and operatic versions, above all Jean Racine's romanticized *Andromaque* (1667), which has dominated most subsequent versions of the story, such as Ambrose Philips' tragedy *The Distrest Mother* (1712), Gioacchino Rossini's opera *Ermione* (1819), Charles Baudelaire's poem "Le Cygne" ("The Swan," 1859), and Craig Raine's drama *1953* (1990). Critics used to complain that Euripides' *Andromache* was poorly constructed and marred by political propaganda, but recently the play has enjoyed a remarkable revival of interest and appreciation.

ANDROMACHE

Characters

ANDROMACHE, Hector's widow; slave and concubine of Achilles' son Neoptolemus
SERVANT WOMAN, formerly Andromache's slave in Troy
CHORUS of Phthian women
HERMIONE, daughter of Menelaus and wife of Neoptolemus
MENELAUS, king of Sparta, father of Hermione
CHILD, son of Andromache and Neoptolemus
PELEUS, father of Achilles, grandfather of Neoptolemus, and husband of Thetis
NURSE, servant of Hermione
ORESTES, son of Agamemnon and Clytemnestra; cousin of Hermione
MESSENGER
THETIS, sea goddess, wife of Peleus and mother of Achilles

Scene: The house of Neoptolemus at Thetideion, near Pharsala in Thessaly; there is an altar and statue of Thetis.

(Enter Andromache from the house. She goes to the altar and sits as a suppliant.)

ANDROMACHE

City of Thebe, Asia's ornament,
from you I once came, my dowry rich in gold
and luxuries, to Priam's royal hearth,

given to Hector as wife, to bear his children.
Andromache was someone to envy, then,
but now: if any woman is unhappy, I am.°
I saw my husband Hector killed by Achilles,
and the son I bore my husband, Astyanax—
I saw him thrown from the steep city walls,
after the Greeks had taken the land of Troy.
From a house most free, I came to Greece a slave,
given to Achilles' son, the islander
Neoptolemus, to be his spear's reward,
a choice selection from the Trojan loot.
I live in these plains, the borderlands of Phthia
by the city of Pharsala; the sea goddess,
Thetis, made her home here with Peleus,
away from humans, shunning the crowd. Thessalians
call it Thetideion after the goddess's wedding.
It is here that the son of Achilles has his home,
letting Peleus rule Pharsala, since he'd rather
not take the scepter while the old man lives.
And in this house I've borne a child, a boy,
after being joined with Achilles' son: my master.
My situation was evil enough before;
still, I always hoped that while my child was safe
I would find some help, some protection against evils.
But since my master married Hermione
the Spartan, and rejected my slave bed,
I am driven by her evil cruelties.
She says that by the use of secret drugs
I make her childless, hateful to her husband;
that I wish to occupy this house myself
in her place, forcing her out of the marriage bed,
a thing I first accepted against my will,
and now have left behind. Great Zeus should know
it was against my will I shared that bed.
But I can't persuade her, and she wants to kill me,
and Menelaus helps his daughter in this.

He is in the house, now, having traveled from Sparta
for this very purpose. In terror I have come
to sit at Thetis' shrine, here by the house,
in the hope it may prevent my being killed—
since Peleus and the descendants of Peleus
respect this symbol of the Nereid's marriage.
I've sent my son, my only child, in secret
to another household, afraid he might be killed.
The one who fathered him isn't here to help me,
and is no use to the boy, since he's away
in Delphi: there he's paying Apollo amends
for the madness that once made him go to Pytho
to ask the god amends for his father's death.
He hopes by asking pardon for those earlier
mistakes to make Apollo kind in future.

(Enter a female Servant from the house.)

SERVANT

Mistress—I don't mind calling you this name,
since I saw fit to do so in your house
when we were still in Troy—I was sympathetic
to you and to your husband, while he lived,
and now I've come to bring you fresh bad news.
I'm afraid that one of my masters will find out,
but I pity you. Menelaus and his daughter
have dreadful plans for you: be on your guard.

ANDROMACHE

Dearest fellow slave—since you are a fellow slave
to me, once queen, now an unlucky woman—
what are they doing? What schemes are they up to now,
wanting to kill me, wretched as I am?

SERVANT

It's your son they mean to kill, unhappy woman,
whom you sent away in secret out of the house.
Menelaus has left the house and gone to get him.°

ANDROMACHE

Oh, no. Has he found the child I sent away?
How could this happen? O misery! I am lost.

SERVANT

I don't know, but this is what I've learned from them.

ANDROMACHE

Then I am lost. Oh child, this pair of vultures
will seize and kill you, while the one they call
your father is still lingering on at Delphi.

SERVANT

Yes, I think you wouldn't be doing so badly
if he were here; as it is, you are without friends.

ANDROMACHE

And Peleus? Is there no report of his coming?

SERVANT

He's too old to help you, even if he were here.

ANDROMACHE

And still I sent for him, and not just once.

SERVANT

You think any of your messengers cared about you?

ANDROMACHE

Why would they? Then—will *you* go take my message?

SERVANT

What shall I say if away from the house too long?

ANDROMACHE

You are a woman: never short of schemes.

SERVANT

It's a risk. Hermione is no mean guard.

ANDROMACHE

See? You deny your friends when times are bad.

SERVANT

Not at all. Don't cast this reproach at me!
I'll go—since the life of a woman who's a slave
is of little concern—whatever evil I suffer.

(Exit Servant to the side.)

ANDROMACHE

Leave, then. And I will stretch out to the sky
the mourning and the wailing and the tears
in which I live. It is natural for women
to take some pleasure in evil circumstances
by keeping them always on the lips and tongue.
I have not one but many things to grieve for:
my father's city, and Hector, who is dead,
and the hard destiny with which I am yoked,
the day of slavery met with undeserved.
You should never speak of any mortal as happy
until he dies and you see how he has passed
his final day and goes beneath the earth.

[*singing*]
To tall Troy Paris brought not marriage but disaster
when he brought Helen to his bedroom there.
For her sake the swift war god and the thousand ships of Greece
took you captive, Troy, with spear and fire,
and to my misery killed my husband Hector. The son of Thetis
dragged him at his chariot wheels around the walls.
Myself: I was led from my rooms to the shore of the sea
covering my head in this slavery I hate.
Many tears ran down my cheeks as I left behind
my city, my rooms, my husband in the dust.
Oh, I am miserable: why should I still see the light
as Hermione's slave? Worn down by her,
I come as a suppliant, arms round the goddess's image,
and pour out my grief like a stream over stone.

(Enter the Chorus of Phthian women from the side.)

CHORUS [singing]

STROPHE A

You have been sitting here, woman, on the floor of Thetis' shrine
a long time, without leaving.
And although I am Phthian and you are a child of Asia, I came
to see if I might find a cure
for the troubles you can't undo
that pit you against Hermione, in hateful competition,
poor woman, over a double
marriage, sharing a single
husband, Achilles' son.

ANTISTROPHE A

Recognize your fate, consider the evils at hand:
you quarrel with your masters
although you are a Trojan girl and they are Sparta's children.
Leave the sea goddess's
sacrificial shrine. What use,
distraught as you are, to do yourself harm by weeping
under your masters' duress?
Their power will overtake you:
why struggle, when you are nothing?

STROPHE B

Come: leave the shining home of the goddess, Nereus' daughter.
Recognize that you are a servant
from a foreign land, in a strange
city, where you see none of your friends:
most unlucky,
utterly wretched bride.

ANTISTROPHE B

To me you seemed truly pitiful when you came, Trojan woman,
to my masters' house. But I
keep quiet, out of fear
(though I pity your situation)

that the child of Zeus' daughter
may find out I wish you well.

(Enter Hermione from the house.)

HERMIONE

The luxurious gold diadem I wear,
the many-colored fabric of my robe:
I didn't bring them here as offerings
from the house of Achilles or of Peleus.
No: they are from Sparta, the Laconian land.
Menelaus my father gave these gifts to me
with an ample dowry, so I am free to speak.
This, then, is how I answer all of you.°
You are a slave, a woman won by the spear,
who wants to keep this home and throw me out.
Your drugs have made me hateful to my husband,
and because of you my ruined womb is barren.
The minds of Asian women are terribly clever
at things like this. But I will make you stop,
and the Nereid's home will be no help at all—
not her altar, not her shrine. No: you will die.
So if some mortal or god is willing to save you,
you must let go your former prosperous pride
to cower in humility, fall at my knee,
sweep my house, sprinkle Achelous' water
over the dust, by hand, from golden jars,
and learn what land you're in. Hector's not here,
nor Priam with his gold: this city's Greek.
Are you so ignorant, you wretched creature,
that you can bear to go to bed with a man
whose father killed your husband, and to have
the killer's children? Barbarians are all like that:
father has sex with daughter, son with mother,
girl with brother, the nearest relatives
murder each other, and no law holds them back.

Don't bring these ways to us. It isn't nice
when one man has two women by the reins;
whoever wants to live in decency
is satisfied with one love in his bed.

CHORUS LEADER

The heart of a woman is a jealous thing,
always most hostile to her fellow wives.

ANDROMACHE

How sad.
Youth's a bad thing for mortals, most of all
when someone young holds fast to what's unjust.
I'm afraid that my position as your slave
will prevent my speaking though I am in the right.
And besides, if I win my case, I'll suffer for it:
those with grand thoughts respond with bitterness
to being out-argued by their inferiors.
Still, I will not be found guilty of self-betrayal.
Tell me, young woman, what solid case could I make
for expelling you from your legitimate marriage?
That Sparta is a lesser city than Troy,
that my fortune outruns yours, and I am free?°
Or is it because I have a young, fresh body,
a great city, and friends, that I'm so confident
as to want to take over your household in your place?
Why? So that I can bear children in your place
as slaves, a wretched weight for me to tow?
Or will the people tolerate my children
as kings of Phthia, if you don't give birth?
Are the Greeks fond of me, for Hector's sake?
Was I obscure, not queen of the Phrygians?
No, it's not my drugs that make your husband hate you:
you have turned out to be unfit to live with.
This is the love charm, woman: it isn't beauty
but goodness that gives pleasure to our husbands.
When you are annoyed by something, you say that Sparta

is great and Scyros nowhere, that you are rich
and they are poor, that Menelaus is greater
than Achilles: this is why your husband hates you.
A woman, even married to an inferior,
must accept him, not compete with him in pride.
If your husband were a king in snowy Thrace,
where a man shares his bed with many wives in turn,
would you have killed them? That would build the case
that every woman is quite insatiable
in bed. A disgrace! Yes, women suffer this sickness
more than men, but still we hide it decently.
My dearest Hector, it's true that for your sake
I helped you in love when Aphrodite tripped you,
and I often nursed your children from other women,
so as not to show any bitterness to you.
In doing so, I drew my husband closer
by my goodness. You're afraid to let a drop
of dew from the open sky come near your husband.
Don't try to outdo your mother in loving men:
sensible children avoid bad mothers' ways.

CHORUS LEADER

Mistress—if this is something you can manage—
do as I say and come to terms with her.

HERMIONE

Why are you arguing so solemnly
that you have self-control and I do not?

ANDROMACHE

To judge from what you just now said, it's true.

HERMIONE

I wouldn't want to live with your kind of sense.

ANDROMACHE

You are young, and you talk about disgraceful things.

HERMIONE

You aren't talking but doing against me all you can.

ANDROMACHE

Can't you just suffer the pain of love in silence?

HERMIONE

Why? Doesn't it come first for women, always?

ANDROMACHE

Yes,
but only for those who treat it decently.

HERMIONE

In this city we don't live under barbarian laws.

ANDROMACHE

Wherever you are, what's shameful causes shame.

HERMIONE

You're wise, so wise. And still you have to die.

ANDROMACHE

Do you see that Thetis' statue stares at you?

HERMIONE

She hates your country because of Achilles' death.

ANDROMACHE

Helen destroyed him: not I, but your mother.

HERMIONE

Are you really going to harp on my misfortunes?

ANDROMACHE

Look: I'm keeping quiet, my mouth's shut tight.

HERMIONE

Just tell me this—the thing I came here for.

ANDROMACHE

I'll tell you this: you lack the sense you need.

HERMIONE

Will you leave the sacred precinct of the sea nymph?

ANDROMACHE

If it doesn't mean death. Otherwise I'll never leave.

HERMIONE

Assume that's settled. I won't wait for my husband.

ANDROMACHE

But I won't give myself up before his return.

HERMIONE

I'll use fire on you, I don't care what happens to you . . .

ANDROMACHE

Well, burn away. The gods will know about it.

HERMIONE

. . . and hurt you with the pain of dreadful wounds.

ANDROMACHE

Slaughter me, bloody the altar; the goddess will punish.

HERMIONE

You barbarian creature, you stubborn piece of boldness,
will you then face down death? I'll make you leave
this sanctuary soon and willingly,
with the bait I have for you. I won't say what,
since the event will reveal it soon enough.
So keep your seat, for even if you were gripped
by molten lead, I will make you leave before
Achilles' son—in whom you trust—returns.

(Exit Hermione into the house.)

ANDROMACHE

I do trust in him. But how terrible it is
that a god gave mortals cures for savage snakes
yet no one has discovered remedies

for something worse than viper, worse than flame:
a bad woman. We bring so much harm to men.°

CHORUS [*singing*]

STROPHE A

The great sorrows had their start when Hermes,
child of Maia and Zeus,
came to a glen on Mount Ida,
bringing a triple team
of goddesses, yoked beauty
armed with a hateful contest (who is fairest?)
to the cattle sheds,
the solitary young herdsman, his
isolated
hearth and home.

ANTISTROPHE A

When they came to the wooded glen they washed
their radiant bodies
in the mountain streams,
went to Priam's son as rivals
in the spiteful excess of their
speeches. Aphrodite won with her crafty words,
delightful to hear
but a bitter life's ruin for the Trojans'
unhappy
city and citadel.

STROPHE B

If only the one who gave birth to him
had cast him away, an evil fate,
before he came to live on rocky Ida.
By her prophetic laurel tree
Cassandra cried out: kill him,
the great disgrace of Priam's city!
Whom did she not approach? Which of the elders
did she not beg to put the baby to death?

ANTISTROPHE B

Slavery's yoke would not have come
to the Trojan women, and you
would have kept your place in the royal house.
She'd have saved Greece from the grief
of the struggle around Troy:
ten years' armed exile of her young men.
The marriage beds would not have been left
deserted, the old not robbed of their children.

(Enter Menelaus from the side, with Andromache's son.)

MENELAUS

I am here, and I've got your child, whom you sent away
to another household without my daughter's knowledge.
You were sure you would be safe with the goddess's image,
the child with those who hid him. But it turns out
you were less clever than Menelaus, woman.
And if you don't get out and abandon this shrine
the child here will be slaughtered in your place.
So think it through: would you prefer to die,
or to have him killed as payment for the crimes
that you are committing against me and my daughter?

ANDROMACHE

Celebrity, celebrity: you inflate
the lives of countless good-for-nothing mortals.
I count as happy those whom truth makes famous,°
but I think unworthy those whose fame's a lie,
though chance may make them seem intelligent.
Are you really the one who led the Greeks' picked men,
and captured Priam's Troy, you nonentity?
a man who at one word from his childish daughter
huffs and puffs, and has plunged into a contest
against a poor slave woman? You are unworthy
of Troy, and Troy, I think, did not deserve you.
Outwardly, those who appear to be intelligent°

may shine, but inside they're just like everyone else,
except for their wealth: that is what has great power.
But come, Menelaus, let's pursue our talk.
Suppose I am dead and your daughter has destroyed me.
She won't escape the stain of bloody murder.
In the eyes of most you too will face that charge:
the accomplice's role makes this inevitable.
And if I myself manage to escape from death,
will you kill my son? Do you suppose his father
will lightly put up with his own child's death?
Troy doesn't give him such a coward's name!
No, he'll go to all lengths, do what he must to show
he's worthy of Peleus and of his father Achilles:
he'll banish your child from his house. And if you give her
to another, what will you tell him? That her virtue
made her shun her wicked husband? He won't believe you.
Who will marry her? Will you keep her at home, bereft
and husbandless till she's gray-haired? Poor man:
can't you see all these evils rushing in?
How many times would you rather find your daughter
mistreated in marriage than suffer what I describe?
You shouldn't cause great evils for small reasons,
nor, if we women are a disastrous evil,
should men become like women in their nature.
If in fact I am giving poisons to your daughter
and making her womb miscarry, as she says,
I am ready and not reluctant to pay the price,
without asking mercy, to your son-in-law,
whom I harm no less by depriving him of children.
This is my position. As for yours, one thing
makes me afraid: a quarrel over a woman
once also led you to destroy poor Troy.

CHORUS LEADER

You have said more than a woman should say to men,
and self-control has flown far from your mind.°

MENELAUS

Woman, these are small matters, as you say,
not worthy of my kingship or of Greece.
But you should know: whatever someone needs
will matter more to him than conquering Troy.
And since I judge this an important loss—
the end of my daughter's marriage—I am her ally.
Other things a woman suffers take second place:
to lose a husband is to lose her life.
And just as Neoptolemus rules over my slaves,
so does my family govern his; I too.
Friends and family have no private property,
if they're true friends, but everything's in common.
And while he's away, and I'm waiting, if I fail
to arrange my affairs for the best, I'm weak, not wise.
Well, get up and leave this temple of the goddess,
since, if you die, this child escapes from death,
but if you don't want to die, then I will kill him.
One of the pair of you must leave this life.

ANDROMACHE

Ah, what a bitter lottery and choice
of life you stage for me, since if I win
I am wretched, and I am luckless if I lose.
You who commit great deeds for little cause,
listen: why kill me? For what? What city have I
betrayed? Which of your children did I kill?
What home did I burn down? Yes, I was forced
to sleep with my master—so you'll kill me, not him,
letting go the cause and dealing with the outcome?
Oh, this ill fortune! My unhappy country,
how terribly I suffer. Why did I give birth
and add another burden to my burden?
But why do I grieve for this, and not drain dry°
and reckon up the evils before me now?
I saw Hector slaughtered, dragged by a chariot's wheels,

and Ilium pitiably set to burn.
I myself, a slave, went down to the Argive ships,
pulled along by the hair. And when I arrived at Phthia,
I was married off to Hector's murderers.
What's sweet for me in life? Where can I look?
to my present fortunes, or the ones gone by?
This child was the one last treasure of my life,
and those with power to choose are about to kill him.
No, he won't die to save my unhappy life!
In him there is hope, if he can still be saved,
but I am disgraced, if I won't die for my child.

(She leaves the altar.)

See, I'm leaving the altar. I am in your hands:
to slaughter, murder, bind, hang by the neck.
My child, I gave you birth; so you may live
I go to Hades. If you escape from death,
remember your mother, and how I endured and died.
And when you go to your father, kissing him,
and shedding tears and putting your arms around him,
tell him what I have done. Children are the soul
of all human beings. Those who haven't any,
and find the idea unpleasant, suffer less,
but theirs is an unlucky happiness.

CHORUS LEADER

I pity you as I listen. Bad luck deserves
pity from all mortals, even for an outsider.
Menelaus: you should have reconciled your daughter
to this woman and found a way out of her troubles.

MENELAUS

Take hold of her, tie her hands behind her back,
servants. She will not like the words she hears.

(The servants do as instructed.)

I've got you! To make you leave the holy altar

of the goddess, I threatened to kill your son, and so
led you to come into my hands for slaughter.
Understand that this is how things are with you.
As for this child—my own child will decide
whether she wishes to kill or not to kill him.
Now go into the house, so you may learn:
once you're a slave, never insult the free.

ANDROMACHE

No. No! You got round me by a trick. I'm cheated!

MENELAUS

Proclaim it to everyone; I won't deny it.

ANDROMACHE

Is this what counts as clever among you Spartans?

MENELAUS

Among the Trojans too: retaliation.

ANDROMACHE

Are the gods no gods? Don't you think they pass judgment?

MENELAUS

When judgment comes, I'll bear it. But I will kill you.

ANDROMACHE

This nestling too, wrenched from beneath my wings?

MENELAUS

No, I'll give him to my daughter, to kill if she likes.

ANDROMACHE

Then why am I not mourning you, my child?

MENELAUS

Indeed, no confident hope awaits him now.

ANDROMACHE

Most hated mortals in the eyes of all,
inhabitants of Sparta, crafty plotters,

lords of the lie, weavers of evil schemes,
with thoughts all twisted, devious, unhealthy,
how unjust your success among the Greeks!
What record don't you hold? The one for murders?
For shameless profiteering? For being caught
saying one thing, with something else in mind?
To hell with you all! For me death's not so hard
as you may think. I died when they destroyed
the unhappy city of Troy and my great husband,
who with his spear so often made you flee
from land to ship, a coward everywhere.
Now, showing yourself a fierce soldier against a woman,
you mean to kill me. Kill! My tongue will speak
no flattery to you or to your daughter:
though you are great in Sparta by your birth,
I was great in Troy. And if my life goes badly
don't boast of this: you may do badly too.

(Exit Menelaus, Andromache, and her son into the house.)

CHORUS [*singing*]

STROPHE A

Never will I approve double marriage for mortals,
sons with different mothers,
rivalry in the house and angry grievances.
May my husband be satisfied
with one
unshared marriage bed.

ANTISTROPHE A

Nor in cities is a twofold tyranny
better to bear than one:
burden on burden, strife among citizens.
And when a pair of craftsmen compose a song,
then conflict
is what the Muses like to create.

STROPHE B

When swift winds carry sailors along,
a double judgment at the helm
and a crowd of wise men have less force
than a simpler mind with power all its own.
Success comes from one, in households
and in cities that look for
a turning point.

ANTISTROPHE B

Proof: the Spartan daughter of general
Menelaus. She came like fire at her rival.
She means to kill the unhappy Trojan girl
and her child in a spiteful contest.
This murder is godless, lawless, graceless.
Mistress, reversal will overtake you
still, for these acts.

(Enter Andromache and her son, bound, and Menelaus holding a sword, from the house.)

[*chanting*]
And now I see   in front of the house
this pair yoked together   under sentence of death;
wretched woman   and you, poor child,
condemned to die   for your mother's marriage,
though you took no part   and bear no guilt
toward our rulers.

ANDROMACHE [*singing throughout the following lyric exchange, as does her Child*]

STROPHE

Here I am, wrists tightly bound
and bloodied by the rope
on my way under ground.

CHILD

Mother, mother,

beneath your wing
I too journey down.

ANDROMACHE
A hateful sacrifice,
you rulers of Phthia.

CHILD
Father, come help
the ones you love!

ANDROMACHE
You will lie, my dear child,
at your mother's breast:
a corpse with a corpse,
underground, at rest.

CHILD
What's happening to me?
Poor me, poor you, mother.

MENELAUS [*chanting*]
Go beneath the earth,   because you came
from an enemy's towers.   The two of you die
by a double necessity: my own vote
does away with you,   my child Hermione's
kills this child.   It is thoughtlessness
of a major kind   to leave enemy children
of enemies behind,   when instead you can kill,
and relieve your household of fear.

ANDROMACHE

ANTISTROPHE

Husband, husband, if only
your hand and spear
could fight for me here, son of Priam!

CHILD
So unhappy: what song
against death can I find?

ANDROMACHE

Pray, cling to your master's
knee, my child.

CHILD (*To Menelaus.*)

Please be my friend.
Do not kill me.

ANDROMACHE

My eyes flow with tears:
like a sunless stream
from a smooth rock: sorrow.

CHILD

Oh, what cure can I find
for the trouble I'm in?

MENELAUS [*again chanting*]

Why fall before me   in supplication?
I am like a rock   in the sea, or a wave.
To my own people   I offer help;
but for you no charm   makes me feel concern,
since in fact I spent   a great part of myself
to take Troy and your mother: so you can thank her
for your journey below, down to Hades.

(*Enter Peleus from the side, accompanied by the Servant.*)

CHORUS LEADER

Wait, I've just caught sight of Peleus nearby,
hurrying here, though with an old man's step.

PELEUS

You there, all of you, and you, the man in charge
of the slaughter: what is this? What's wrong with the household?
What are you doing, scheming without a trial?
Menelaus, stop; don't hurry things unjustly.

(To the Servant.)

You, lead me faster, since it seems events
allow no leisure, but mean I must regain
now if ever the strength I had when young.
First I'll fill this woman's sails with a fair wind.
Tell me, by what right are they leading you
and the child away, your hands bound tight with rope?
You're being killed here like a ewe with her lamb
while I am absent, and your master too.

ANDROMACHE [*now speaking*]
Old man, they are taking me away to die,
with the child, just as you see. What can I say?
Not with the eagerness of a single summons
but by countless messengers I sent for you.
I suppose you have heard of the conflict this man's daughter
has caused in the house, and why I am being killed.
And now they've dragged me from the shrine of Thetis,
who bore you a noble son, and whom you revere,
and are leading me away, judged without trial.
They didn't wait for those who are absent from home,
but knowing my isolation and this child's
(although he is guiltless) they intend to kill him,
along with my unhappy self. But I beg you,
old man, falling at your knees, since I can't reach
your dear chin with my hand: Rescue me, by the gods!
If not, we die—your disgrace and my misfortune.

PELEUS *(To the servants holding Andromache and her son.)*
I order you to undo these bonds and release
this woman's hands, before someone suffers for it.

MENELAUS
And I forbid it—second to you in nothing,
and with much more authority over this woman.

PELEUS

What? Are you planning to come and run my house?
Isn't it enough for you to rule in Sparta?

MENELAUS

It was I that took her prisoner from Troy!

PELEUS

It was my son's son that got her as his prize.

MENELAUS

Isn't what's mine his, and isn't what's his mine?

PELEUS

Yes,
to treat well, not badly—and not to kill.

MENELAUS

You will never take this woman from my hands.

PELEUS

Yes, I will, after my scepter has bloodied your head.

MENELAUS

Touch me, and you'll find out. Go on, come close.

PELEUS

Are you a man, you coward and child of cowards?
Do men consider you as one of them?
A Phrygian relieved you of your wife
when you went away and left her room unlocked,
unguarded, as if you had a modest wife,
when in fact she was the worst. Even if she wished,
no Spartan girl could ever turn out modest:
abandoning their homes, and with bare thighs
and loosened cloaks they share the stadiums
and wrestling halls—a thing I can't tolerate—
with the young men. So is it any wonder
that you don't raise your women to be modest?
Ask Helen this, since she left home and family

to run off with a young man to another land.
And then because of her you brought together
so great a crowd of Greeks to lead to Troy?
You knew she was bad: you should have spat her out,
not taken up your spear, but left her there
and paid a fee never to bring her home.
But that was not the way you set your mind,
and you brought many brave souls to destruction
and made old women childless in their chambers
and took from gray-haired fathers noble sons.
I am one of them, to my sorrow. I look at you
as Achilles' murderer, as a pollution.
You alone came from Troy without a wound;
you took there and brought home again untouched
the finest armor in fine coverings.
I told my grandson, when he planned to marry,
to form no alliance with you, not to take home
a bad woman's filly: they bring along with them
the mother's faults. I warn you, suitors, look closely,
and get yourself the daughter of a good mother.
  What an outrage you inflicted on your brother,
telling him to sacrifice his daughter—such folly!
Were you so afraid to lose your wicked wife?
And when you took Troy—yes, I'll speak of that—
and caught your worthless wife, you didn't kill her.
No, when you saw her breast, you threw down your sword
and kissed her, fawning on the treacherous bitch,
overcome by Aphrodite—you disgusting man!
Then you come to my son's house, to plunder it
in his absence, and to kill an unhappy woman—
shamelessly!—and a boy, who will make you suffer
for what you've done, and your daughter in there too,
even if he's triply a bastard. Often enough
dry ground outdoes deep soil in the seed it bears,
and often bastards are better than true-born sons.
Take your daughter away. Mortals are better off

with a poor but honest father-in-law and friend
than a worthless one who is wealthy. You are nothing.

CHORUS LEADER

From a small beginning speech can bring about
serious dissension. Mortals who are wise
are wary of causing conflict with their friends.

MENELAUS

Why should we attribute wisdom to old men
and to those who once seemed prudent to the Greeks,
when you, Peleus, born of a famous father,
and joined with us by marriage, disgrace yourself
and censure us for this barbarian woman?
You should be driving her off beyond the Nile,
or beyond the Phasis, and calling on me to help:
she is from Asia, where so many Greeks
have fallen by the spear, have fallen dead.
And she has a share in the blood of your own son,
since Paris, who struck down your son Achilles,
was Hector's brother, and she was Hector's wife.
Yet you live under the same roof with this woman,
and think it right for her to share your table,
and have children, our worst enemies, in the house.
When, out of concern for both of us, old man,
I try to kill her, she's snatched from out of my hands.
Come, there's no shame in touching on this point:
if my daughter doesn't give birth, and children are born
from this woman, will you make them kings of Phthia?
And will they, although they are barbarians,
rule over Greeks? Am I unreasonable
in hating injustice? Is good sense on your side?
Consider this: if you had given your daughter°
to a fellow citizen who did this to her,
would you sit by in silence? I think not.
Yet you shout at your relatives over a foreigner?
A man and a woman may feel equal grief,

she if her husband wrongs her, and he likewise
if he has a promiscuous woman in his house.
But he at least has power in his own hands,
while her affairs rely on friends and parents.
So am I not justified in helping my own?
You are an old, old man. And when you speak
of my leadership, that helps me more than silence.
Helen's troubles came from the gods: she didn't choose them,
and her suffering did the Greeks the greatest good.
Ignorant of weapons and of battle,
they went on to fight bravely; yes, experience
is a general education for mortal men.
And if, when I came to gaze upon my wife,
I held back from killing her, that was self-restraint.
I would prefer that *you* had not murdered Phocus!
I've gone after you like this out of goodwill,
not out of anger. If you lose your temper,
you wear out your voice: but my foresight profits me.

CHORUS LEADER

Here is my best advice: put a stop, now,
to this pointless exchange, so both of you don't lose.

PELEUS

How bad the current custom is in Greece!
When an army triumphs over its enemies,
they don't count this the deed of those who worked
and suffered; no, the general wins the glory.
One among countless others he waves his spear,
and does no more than one, but gets more credit.
Sitting solemnly in office they think bigger thoughts°
than the common people, although they are nobodies.
But if the people could only plan and dare,
they would be a thousand times wiser than the great.
So you and your brother sit, swollen with pride
about Troy and about your leadership over there,
exalted by the painful struggles of others.

I'll teach you never to consider Paris
of Ida a greater enemy than Peleus
if you don't get away from this place at once
along with your childless daughter—whom my grandson
will take by the hair and hurry through the house.
Barren heifer that she is, she can't tolerate
others giving birth, while she has no young herself.
Just because your daughter is unlucky with children,
does she have to deprive us of our own offspring too?
Get away from her, servants, so I can find out
if anyone will prevent my freeing her hands.

(To Andromache.)

Lift yourself up—since, although I am trembling,
I will undo these knotted leather straps.

(To Menelaus.)

Is this how you abused her hands, you coward?
Did you think to tighten the noose on a bull or a lion?
Or were you afraid that she would seize a sword
and fight you off? Come here, child, to my arms,
help me undo your mother's bonds. I'll raise you
in Phthia to be a great enemy to them. You Spartans:
apart from your reputation as great warriors,
in other things you're no better than anyone else.

CHORUS LEADER

Old men lack self control, and since they're quick
to anger they are difficult to deal with.

MENELAUS

You are too prone to abuse. But since I came
to Phthia because I had to, I will neither
commit nor suffer any shabby treatment.
And now—since I don't have plenty of time to spare—
I'm going to head for home. There is a city,
not far from Sparta, which used to be our friend

and now is hostile. I mean to lead my army
against it, attack, and get it under control.
When I've arranged things there as I judge best,
I'll return, and face-to-face my son-in-law
and I will have a candid exchange of words.
And if he punishes her, and for the future
acts toward us with restraint, he will meet restraint.
But if he is angry, he will find us angry;
his actions will get reactions in return.°
As for your talk, it doesn't bother me.
You stand here like a shadow with a voice,
incapable of anything save speech.

(Exit Menelaus to the side.)

PELEUS

Come here, child, take my arm and be my guide;
and you, poor woman. You met with a savage storm
but have come to a harbor sheltered from the wind.

ANDROMACHE

Old man, may the gods do well by you and yours,
since you have saved my child and my luckless self.
But watch out: they may yet lie hidden in ambush
where the road is deserted, and carry me off by force,
seeing that you are old, and I am weak,
and my son here is only a child. Take care
that we don't escape now only to be caught later.

PELEUS

No, don't bring in that cowardly woman's talk!
Go on! Who can touch you? He'll be sorry he tried.
With the help of the gods, I'm in command in Phthia
over many hoplites and a mass of cavalry.
And I am still upright, not ancient as you think:
I only have to look at a man like him
to turn him to flight, although I am his elder.

A man of good courage, even if old, gets the better
of many young men, and strength doesn't help a coward.

(Exit Peleus, Andromache, her son, and Servant to the side.)

CHORUS [*singing*]

STROPHE

Either no life, or one with noble ancestors
who belong to a wealthy house.
Help is at hand in any predicament
for the wellborn.
Glory and honor come to those
proclaimed as nobility, and time can't take away
what brave men leave behind; their courage
gleams even when they are gone.

ANTISTROPHE

Better to gain a victory without dishonor
than to overthrow justice with envious force;
that is sweet in the moment to mortals,
but in time it withers
and the house is wrapped in blame.
This, this is the life I praise and take for my own:
to hold no power beyond what's just
at home or in the city.

EPODE

Old son of Aeacus,
I can believe you joined the Lapiths
to battle the Centaurs with your far-famed spear
and on the Argo passed through the unfriendly waters
of the sea's Clashing Rocks
on that famous expedition.
And when Heracles first overwhelmed with slaughter
the glorious city of Troy,
you returned to Europe with your share of fame.

(Enter Hermione's Nurse from the house.)

NURSE

Dearest women, how evil follows evil
today, one thing right after the other. So now
my mistress in the house, Hermione,
deserted by her father, and aware
of what she has done—the plan she made to kill
Andromache and her son—wishes to die.
She is frightened of her husband, fears her acts
may lead to her dismissal and disgrace
or to her facing death for attempted murder.°
The slaves that watch over her could hardly keep her
from hanging herself; they had to seize the sword
from her right hand and take it away from her.
That's how remorseful she is over what she has done;
she knows she acted badly. As for me, friends,
I am tired of keeping my mistress from the noose.
But you can make your way inside this house
and rescue her from death, since newcomers
are more persuasive than familiar friends.

(Shouts are heard from within the house.)

CHORUS LEADER

Yes, we can hear the attendants in the house
making an outcry about what you reported.

(Enter Hermione from the house.)

The poor woman will show, it seems, how much she grieves
for the horrors she committed: here she comes,
evading her servants' hands, longing to die.

HERMIONE [*singing, while the Nurse speaks in reply*]

STROPHE A

I can't bear it.
I'll tear my hair and scratch
my face with savage nails!

NURSE

What are you doing? Disfiguring yourself?

HERMIONE

ANTISTROPHE A

Aah, aah!
Off my hair, into the sky,
veil of delicate threads!

NURSE

Cover your breasts, child, pull your dress together!

HERMIONE

STROPHE B

Why cover my breasts with my dress?
What I have done to my husband
is plain, clear, unconcealed.

NURSE

You're sorry you planned to murder your fellow wife?

HERMIONE

ANTISTROPHE B

Yes: I grieve for my recklessness
and my savagery, cursed,
cursed for what I did.

NURSE

Your husband will pardon you for this mistake.

HERMIONE

Why hunt the sword from my hand?
Give it back, friend, so I may strike!
Why keep me from the noose?

NURSE

But what if I let you die while out of your mind?

HERMIONE

Oh, my fate.

Where is fire's dear flame for me?
Where can I leap from a rock
into sea or mountain wood,
to die and belong to the dead?

NURSE

Why do you struggle? Misfortunes sent by god
come to all mortals at one time or another.

HERMIONE

You left me, you left me, father,
alone on the shore with no ship.
He'll kill me, my husband, that's clear.
He'll kill me. No more life
in this bridal chamber for me.
What god shall I run to and beg?
Shall I bow to my slave as a slave?
If only I were a bird,
dark winged, in flight from Phthia,
where the pinewood ship passed through
the darkling promontories,
its oars still new to the sea.

NURSE

My child, I thought you went too far before
when you acted wrongly toward the Trojan woman,
and now you go too far in what you fear.
Your husband won't rely on the worthless words
of a barbarian wife and reject your marriage.
You're no war captive from the sack of Troy,
but the child of a noble father, and he got you
with a plentiful dowry from a prosperous city.
Your father hasn't betrayed you as you fear,
and he won't let you be banished from your home.
Now go inside and don't make a display
in front of the house; you could disgrace yourself
by being seen out here in front of these halls.°

CHORUS LEADER *(Enter Orestes from the side.)*

Yes, and here comes a foreign-looking stranger;
He's making his way toward us in a hurry.

ORESTES

Women of Phthia, is this in fact the home
of Achilles' son? Is this the royal house?

CHORUS LEADER

It is. But who are you to ask this question?

ORESTES

The son of Agamemnon and Clytemnestra,
Orestes. I'm on my way to the oracle
of Zeus at Dodona, and since I've come to Phthia,
I thought I'd try to find out about a woman,
a relative of mine, Hermione the Spartan,
whether she is alive and well—for though she lives
far away from me, I am still fond of her.

(Hermione kneels before Orestes as a suppliant.)

HERMIONE

You appear as a harbor to sailors in storm,
Agamemnon's child, and at your knees I beg you:
pity me for the terrible circumstances
you see me in. I put my arms around
your knees, as if I held out suppliant branches.

ORESTES

Wait,
what's this? Am I wrong, or do I really see
the queen of this household, Menelaus' daughter?

HERMIONE

Yes—the only child that Tyndareus' daughter,
Helen, had with my father. You're not mistaken.

ORESTES

Phoebus the healer, grant release from pain!
What's the trouble? Does it come from gods or mortals?

HERMIONE

From myself, and from the husband who married me,
and from some god. I am ruined on every side.

ORESTES

What problem could a woman face who has
no children yet—unless it involves her marriage?

HERMIONE

You bring me to the point: that's just my trouble.

ORESTES

Does your husband love another in your place?

HERMIONE

His concubine, the captive, Hector's wife.

ORESTES

That's a bad thing—two bedmates for one man.

HERMIONE

That's how it is. So then I defended myself.

ORESTES

You didn't plot against her, as women do?

HERMIONE

Yes: death for her and for her bastard child.

ORESTES

Did you kill them, or did some chance rescue them?

HERMIONE

It was old man Peleus, honoring inferiors.

ORESTES

Was anyone your accomplice in this murder?

HERMIONE
My father, who came from Sparta with this aim.

ORESTES
And then was beaten by an old man's strength?

HERMIONE
Yes, out of respect. And went off abandoning me.

ORESTES
I see: you fear your husband for what you've done.

HERMIONE
Yes: he would be right to kill me. What can I say?
But I beg you, by Zeus, the god of family,
escort me as far from this land as possible,
or to my father's hall—since it seems to me
this house has taken a voice and drives me out,
and the land of Phthia hates me. If my husband
leaves the Delphic oracle and gets home first,
he will kill me in disgrace, or I will serve
as a slave the bastard bed I ruled before.
So how did I—as some might say—go wrong?°
Visits from bad women ruined me.
They talked to me like this and made me vain:
"Will you allow the lowest household slave,
captured in battle, to share a bed with you?
By Hera, in my house she wouldn't live
to see the light if she enjoyed my bed."
And when I listened to these Sirens' words,
their clever, roguish, subtle chattering,°
I was puffed up with folly. Why did I need
to watch my husband, when I had everything?
I was very wealthy, and I ruled the house;
any children I had would be legitimate,
her children bastards and half-slaves to mine.
But never, never—I'll say it not just once—
should any married man who has good sense

allow other women to come visiting
his wife at home: they'll teach her wickedness.
One will destroy the marriage for some profit,
another has gone wrong and wants company,
and many are wild for sex. So husbands' homes
fall ill. In face of this you ought to guard
the gates of your houses well, with bolts and bars,
for women's visits from outside result
in nothing healthy, just many kinds of trouble.

CHORUS LEADER

You speak too freely against your fellow women—
forgivable in you, perhaps, but still,
women should cover up other women's failings.

ORESTES

He gave us wise advice, the man who taught
that we should listen to what our enemies say.
I knew of the confusion in this house,
and the quarrel between you and Hector's wife,
so I waited and kept watch: would you stay here,
or, scared at the thought of the captive woman's murder,°
would you consent to be set free from this house?
I didn't defer to your commands, but came,°
so that if you would let me speak, as you have, I could
escort you from this house. You were mine before;
you live with this man because your father's a coward.
Before he made his way across Troy's borders
he gave you to me as wife, then offered you later
to your present husband, if he would sack that city.
And when Achilles' son came home again,
I forgave your father, but I begged your husband
to dissolve your marriage. I spoke of my misfortunes,
and of my present fate: how I could marry
within my family, not easily from outside,
since I am a fugitive, exiled from my home.
But he was insulting, and condemned me for

my mother's murder and the Furies' bloody gaze.
And I, brought down by what had happened at home,
was in anguish—in anguish!—but I endured misfortune,
and went away, without you, unwillingly.
So now, since your situation is reversed
and you have helplessly fallen into misfortune,
I'll bring you home and give you back to your father.
Family's a powerful thing, and in bad times,
nothing is better than a friend from home.

HERMIONE

As for my marriage, that's my father's concern,
and it's not my place to come to this decision.
Just take me out of this house as fast as you can
so my husband doesn't get home first and catch me,
or old Peleus learn that I'm deserting this household
and drive his horses in pursuit of me.

ORESTES

Face down the old man's power. Don't be afraid
of Achilles' son, however he has abused me.
I have contrived a hunting net for him,
and it stands fixed, its mesh unalterable:
death at this hand. I won't speak of it before,
but the Delphic rock will know when it is done.
And if my Pythian allies' oaths hold good,
then I, the matricide, will demonstrate
that he shouldn't have married someone who was mine.
A bitter outcome for his charge of murder
against the lord Apollo! His change of mind
will do no good now he pays that god the price.
At the god's hand and through my accusations
he will die a bad death, and know my enmity.
A god turns over the fate of his enemies
to ruin and doesn't tolerate their pride.

(Exit Orestes, Hermione, and the Nurse to the side.)

CHORUS [*singing*]

STROPHE A

Phoebus, who fortified Troy's rock with walls and towers,
and you, sea god, who drive dark mares
over the salt expanse:
why did you hand over
the dishonored product of your craft
to the war god, master of the spear,
and give up
unhappy, unhappy Troy?

ANTISTROPHE A

You yoked many fine horse-drawn chariots on the banks
of the Simois, and set murderous
contests of men,
no wreath as prize.
The kings of Ilium are dead and gone.
No longer does the altar fire shine out
in Troy, its smoke
fragrant with incense.

STROPHE B

Atreus' son is gone by the cunning of his wife
and she in turn has found death,
murdered by her children.
It was a god, a god's oracular command°
that turned against her: Agamemnon's son
came from the shrine, journeyed on to Argos,
and killed her, murdered his mother.
O god, O Phoebus, how can I believe?

ANTISTROPHE B

In the Greeks' assemblies many laments were sung°
for unlucky children, and wives
left their homes
for another bedmate. Not on you alone
and on your friends did grief and sorrow fall.
Greece endured a plague, a true plague. The storm from Troy

crossed even to her fruitful fields
dripping blood on the children of Danaus.°

(Enter Peleus from the side.)

PELEUS
Women of Phthia, answer what I ask.
I heard a story—but it wasn't clear—
that the daughter of Menelaus has left this house
and is gone. So I have come here, very eager
to find out if it's true. When friends are away,
those at home must take pains in their interest.

CHORUS LEADER
You have heard correctly, Peleus. It's not right
for me to hide the troubles I've been close to.
Our queen is gone, a fugitive from this house.

PELEUS
What was she afraid of? Tell me everything.

CHORUS LEADER
She feared her husband would turn her out of the house.

PELEUS
Because she planned the murder of his child?

CHORUS LEADER
Yes, and the murder of the captive woman.

PELEUS
Did she leave the house with her father—or with whom?

CHORUS LEADER
Agamemnon's son has taken her, and is gone.

PELEUS
Hoping for what? Does he want to marry her?

CHORUS LEADER
Yes, by arranging the death of your son's son.

PELEUS

By an ambush, or will he fight him face-to-face?

CHORUS LEADER

In Loxias' holy shrine, with the Delphians.

PELEUS

No! This is dreadful. Someone must set off
as soon as possible to the Pythian hearth
and tell our friends there what is going on here
before his enemies kill Neoptolemus.

(Enter Messenger from the side.)

MESSENGER

Oh, no. Oh, no.
What news I bring—a wretched messenger—
to you, old man, and to my master's friends.

PELEUS

Aah. My prophetic heart expects disaster.

MESSENGER

He's dead, your grandson, that's the news I bring,
old Peleus: it was the sword blows he received
from the Delphians and their Mycenaean guest.

CHORUS LEADER *(To Peleus.)*

Ah, wait, what are you doing, old man? Don't fall.
Lift yourself up.

PELEUS

I am nothing. I am destroyed.
My voice is gone, my limbs beneath me gone.

MESSENGER

If you really want to help the ones you love,
raise yourself upright, and listen to what happened.

PELEUS

O fate, at the farthest limits of old age
how you have wrapped me round in misery.
How did my only son's only son die?
Tell me. What shouldn't be heard I still wish to hear.

MESSENGER

When we came to the famous precinct of Apollo,
we spent three shining orbits of the sun
devoting ourselves to the sights. Apparently
this seemed suspicious, and the inhabitants,
the god's own people, began to gather in groups.
And Agamemnon's son went through the city
saying malevolent words in each man's ear:
"Do you see this person who goes through the god's precincts,
filled with the gold of mortals' treasuries?
He is here a second time for the same purpose
as before: he wants to sack the temple of Phoebus."
At this, an angry uproar spread through the city
and the council rooms were filled with magistrates
while those in charge of the god's property
privately set guards on the colonnaded temples.
But we, as yet knowing nothing, took some sheep
that were raised for sacrifice in Parnassus' groves,
and went and stood by the altar for offerings
with our sponsors and the Pythian diviners.
And someone said, "Young man, what prayer should we make
to the god on your behalf? What have you come for?"
And he said, "I want to offer compensation
to Phoebus for the wrong I did before,
when I demanded he pay for my father's blood."
And that's when it became clear that Orestes' story—
that my master was lying, and his purpose shameful—
had made its mark. Neoptolemus climbed the steps
and went in, so that he could pray to Phoebus

before the shrine; he was making burnt offerings.
A group of swordsmen was lying in wait for him,
shadowed by the laurel, and Clytemnestra's son
was one of them: he had devised all this.
Neoptolemus stood in full sight and prayed to the god,
while they crept up stealthily with sharpened swords
and stabbed Achilles' son, who wore no armor.
He backed away. His wound, as it turned out,
was not mortal, and he drew his sword, then seized
armor hanging on a peg beside the doorpost
and stood at the altar, a soldier, grim to look at.
He shouted to the sons of Delphi, asking:
"Why are you killing me, here on a pious errand?
What have I done that you should murder me?"
But none of the countless people standing by
said anything in reply: instead, they stoned him.
Pelted by this dense hail on every side
he put forward his weapons to guard against attack
and held his shield out, now this way, now that.
They had no success, and all those many missiles—
arrows, javelins, two-pronged spits pulled out
from sacrificed oxen—fell before his feet.
You would have seen your child warding off spears
in a dreadful Pyrrhic dance. They hemmed him in
from every side and gave him no breathing space.
Abandoning the sacrificial altar,
and leaping as his father did at Troy,
he went for his attackers. Just like doves
that see a hawk, they turned their backs and fled.
Many fell in confusion, some from wounds he gave them,
and others trampled in the narrow exits.
An unholy screaming in the house of holy silence
resounded from the rocks. Somehow in calm
my master stood, gleaming in his bright arms,
until some voice, from the middle of the shrine,
gave a strange and frightening cry, and roused the people,

turning them to strength. Then Achilles' son
fell, struck in the ribs with a sharpened sword
by a Delphian: the one who was his death,°
along with many others. As he fell to the ground,
who didn't attack with iron, or with rock,
hitting and striking? So all his lovely body
was wasted and destroyed by savage wounds.
He lay there a corpse, beside the altar; then
they threw him outside the incense-welcoming shrine.
We took him up in our arms as soon as we could
and we bring him to you, to grieve for and to mourn
with tears, old man, and to honor with burial.
This is what the lord who prophesies to others,
who determines justice for all human beings,
did to Achilles' son, when he came to atone.
Just like a petty human, the god remembered
old, bygone quarrels. How can he be wise?

(Enter a funeral procession carrying Neoptolemus' body from the side.)

CHORUS [*chanting*]

And now our king, carried here
from the land of Delphi, draws near his home.
Unhappy victim, and you old man
unhappy as well. You welcome Achilles'
young cub to your house, not as you would wish.
By your sorrow you join in his fate.°

PELEUS [*singing this ode, as does the Chorus in reply, while the Chorus Leader speaks*]

STROPHE A

I can't bear it. To see this evil fortune,
to take it with my hands into my own home!
The pain! The pain!
City of Thessaly, we are destroyed.
We are gone. No more family, no children left in my house.
Suffering and despair are all I have.

What friend can I look to for cheer?
Dear mouth, dear cheek, dear hands:
if only a god had killed you in battle
at Troy along the banks of the Simois!

CHORUS LEADER

He would have been honored had he died that way,
old man, and you would have been more fortunate.

PELEUS

ANTISTROPHE A

O marriage, marriage that ruined
this home and ruined my city.
Aah aah my child.
If only the hope of children and family°
had not led us into that ill-omened marriage:
Hermione was death to you, my child.
If only she had died, lightning-struck,
and you had not blamed (mortal against god)
Apollo's deadly archery
for your godlike father's blood.

CHORUS

STROPHE B

Sorrow, sorrow: I begin the lament for my master
in the strain that belongs to the dead.

PELEUS

Sorrow, sorrow: In tears I take my turn,
poor unfortunate old man.

CHORUS LEADER

It was god that decreed, god that ordained disaster.

PELEUS

My dear, you deserted the house°
forsaking a childless old man.

CHORUS LEADER

You should have died, old man, before your children.

PELEUS

Should I not tear my hair,
Should I not beat
my head with murderous force? O city,
Phoebus has taken two children from me now.

CHORUS

ANTISTROPHE B

Unhappy old man: you have seen and suffered such evils.
What life can you have left?

PELEUS

Childless, bereft, without end to my misfortunes,
I will drink down trouble till death.

CHORUS LEADER

An empty happiness, your god-sent marriage.

PELEUS

All that has flown away and is gone
far from my lofty boasts.

CHORUS LEADER

You live alone now in a lonely house.

PELEUS

I no longer have a city.
Down with my scepter.
And you, Nereus' daughter, in your night-dark
caves, will see my fall, my utter ruin.

(Enter Thetis above the house.)

CHORUS [*chanting*]

Ah!
What was it that moved?   What divinity
do I sense?   Girls: look, watch closely:
some god carried here   through the clear sky
comes to Phthia, pastureland of horses.

THETIS

Peleus: because I once was married to you,
I, Thetis, have come here, leaving Nereus' house.
And first I advise you not to take too hard
your present evil fortunes. Even I
who never should have shed tears for my children—
since I am a goddess and my father is a god—°
I lost the swift-footed son I had from you,
Achilles, born to be the first in Greece.
I will tell you why I came; listen to my words.
Take this dead man, Achilles' son, and make
your way to the Pythian hearth, and bury him there,
a reproach to the Delphians: the tomb will tell
his violent murder by Orestes' hand.
His captive wife, I mean Andromache,
must join with Helenus in marriage now
and settle in Molossia, old man,
along with this child, the only one remaining
of Aeacus' line. His descendants will pass their lives
one after another, as kings of Molossia,
in prosperity. Your race and mine, old man,
is not to be so utterly uprooted,
nor is that of Troy. The gods do care for her
although she fell by Athena's eager wish.
As for you, so you'll be grateful for our marriage,
I'll free you from the troubles mortals are heir to,
and make you immortal, a god who never fades.
Then, for the future, you will live with me
in Nereus' home, a god beside a goddess.
And with dry foot you will travel out of the sea
to see your dearest child, and mine, Achilles:
he lives in his island home, along the shore
of Leuke in the inhospitable strait.
But now go to Delphi, city built by a god,
taking this body, and after you bury him, come
to the hollow cave on Sepias' ancient headland.

Sit there and wait until I come from the sea
bringing my chorus of fifty Nereids
to accompany you; for this is what is fated,
and you must accept it. Zeus has decided so.
Stop grieving on behalf of those who have died,
since this is the decree the gods have ordained
for all human beings, and death is what they owe.

(Exit Thetis.)

PELEUS

My lady, noble companion of my bed,
offspring of Nereus, greetings. What you do
is worthy of yourself and of your descendants.
At your command I will stop grieving, goddess.
I will bury him, and go to the glens of Pelion
where I first took you—the fairest—in my arms.
Isn't it true that a man who makes sound plans°
should take his wife from a noble family,
give his daughters in marriage to good men,
and not be eager for worthless marriages
even if they bring opulent dowries to the house?
For then the gods will never treat them badly.°

(Exit Peleus, Messenger, and the funeral procession to the side.)

CHORUS [*chanting*]

Divinities take on many forms;°
the gods accomplish much that's unhoped-for.
What we expect goes unfulfilled
and god finds a way for the unexpected.
Such was the outcome of this matter.

HECUBA

Translated by WILLIAM ARROWSMITH

HECUBA: INTRODUCTION

The Play: Date and Composition

It is not certain when Euripides' *Hecuba* was first produced, but metrical considerations suggest a date of around 424 BCE. Presumably Euripides wrote it for the annual competition at the Great Dionysian Festival in Athens. What the other three plays were in Euripides' tetralogy of that year, and how they fared in the dramatic competition, are unknown.

The Myth

Euripides' *Hecuba* combines two stories from the fall of Troy, both involving the sufferings of its last queen, Hecuba. First her daughter Polyxena is sacrificed by the Greeks to the dead Achilles. Then she learns that her youngest son Polydorus, who had been entrusted for safekeeping to the Thracian king Polymestor, has instead been treacherously murdered by him. Hecuba avenges herself upon Polymestor by blinding him and killing his children; at the end it is foretold that she will be transformed into a dog.

The bloody aftermath of the Trojan War—including the Greeks' sacrifice of Polyxena—was recounted in ancient Greek legend in gruesome detail and was often depicted in ancient Greek art. Euripides himself dramatized these events repeatedly, for example in *Andromache* (written only a year or two before *Hecuba*) and *The Trojan Women* (written less than ten years after *Hecuba*). Of the two stories that make up this play, the one involving Polyxena is likely to have been well known to Euripides' audience from heroic myth and epic poetry, though her willingness to be put to death is a characteristically Euripidean motif and may well have been a surprising innovation. By contrast, there is no trace of anything like Euripides' version of the Polydorus story before this play. In Homer, Polydorus is the youngest son of Priam; however, his mother is not Hecuba but Laothoe, another wife of Priam, and the boy is killed in battle by Achilles. Polymestor does not appear anywhere in Greek legend or art before this play, and his etymologically transparent name ("much-planning") suggests that Euripides may well have invented his character and the whole story that centers on him and Polydorus.

Ancient scholars noted that the story of Polyxena was to be found also in a tragedy by Sophocles titled *Polyxena*. While we do not know the date of this play and only very few fragments of it have survived, it seems to have borne a certain degree of resemblance to Euripides' *Hecuba*. Modern scholars disagree about which play came first and whether, if Sophocles' play preceded Euripides', the older playwright might have influenced Euripides' version of the Polyxena story.

Transmission and Reception

There is plenty of evidence that *Hecuba* was quite popular throughout antiquity, including quotations and allusions by later authors and the survival of at least ten papyri containing fragments of the play. It not only was selected as one of the ten canonical plays most studied and read in antiquity, but together with *Orestes* and *The Phoenician Women* it was included in the so-called Byzantine triad. As a result, it is transmitted by hundreds of medieval manuscripts and is equipped with very full ancient and medieval commentaries. Greek and Latin authors who portrayed Hecuba's sufferings after the fall of Troy inevitably drew upon this play and upon Euripides' *Trojan Women*. Narrative poets like Virgil, Ovid, and Quintus of Smyrna (the Greek author of an epic about the events in the Trojan War that occurred after the end of the *Iliad*; probably late fourth century CE) followed the outlines of Euripides' plot at least in part and presumed their readers' familiarity with his text. The Latin dramatists Ennius, in his tragedy *Hecuba*, and Pacuvius, in his tragedy *Ilione* (both plays are lost), seem to have taken Euripides' play as their model; so too Seneca, in his *Trojan Women*, which has been preserved; and Hecuba eventually became a widely recognized figure of the vicissitudes of fortune. In ancient art, the sacrifice of Polyxena is often represented, other scenes that can be connected with Euripides' *Hecuba* much less so.

The popularity of *Hecuba* in the Greek Middle Ages and the fact that its title is alphabetically the first in the Byzantine triad meant that it was usually the first play of Euripides to be read in medieval Byzantium as well as in the West during the Renaissance. As early as the fourteenth century, the first part of the Greek play was accompanied by an interlinear Latin translation, intended to make the play more accessible, that scholars attribute to Leonzio Pilato, who taught Greek to Petrarch and Boccaccio; and a number of other Latin translations survive, starting in the fifteenth century and culminating in Erasmus' successful metrical version. In the same century, Latin and then vernacular translations began to proliferate; and by the sixteenth century *Hecuba* was the most translated and imitated Greek play of all. Euripides' play was especially admired for its demonstration of the mutability of human circumstances, for its careful dramatic construction, for the polished eloquence of its speeches, and for its excessive violence. For the authors and audiences of Elizabethan and Jacobean revenge tragedies, *Hecuba* was a particularly compelling study of the nature and limits of vengeance. So too, the sacrifice of Polyxena fascinated many European painters starting in the seventeenth century (Pietro da Cortona, before 1625; Nicolas Poussin, ca. 1645–50; Giovanni Francesco Romanelli; Luca Giordano; Giovanni Battista Pittoni).

But by the beginning of the nineteenth century *Hecuba* had entered a period of prolonged disparagement and neglect. August Wilhelm Schlegel's influential Vienna lectures *On Dramatic Art and Literature* (1808) established a view of the play as the worst tragedy by the worst Greek tragedian—indeed as the worst surviving Greek tragedy of all—that dominated for more than a century. The play's portrayal of unrelieved suffering, its lyric excesses, the balanced rhetoric of its speeches, and its claustrophobic focus on Hecuba were regarded as intolerable weaknesses. It required considerable changes in classical scholarship, in modern drama, and not least in our sense of the world as a whole, changes characteristic of the second half of the twentieth century, before *Hecuba* could come back into its own. Only recently has this tragedy begun to recover its prominence, both in the estimation of scholars and as a dramatic force in the theater—and largely because of the very same features that nineteenth-century readers had scorned.

HECUBA

Characters

GHOST OF POLYDORUS, son of Hecuba
HECUBA, queen of Troy
CHORUS of captive Trojan women
POLYXENA, daughter of Hecuba
ODYSSEUS, a Greek leader
TALTHYBIUS, herald of the Greeks
HANDMAID of Hecuba
AGAMEMNON, commander in chief of the Greeks at Troy
POLYMESTOR, king of Thracian Chersonese
SONS of Polymestor (silent characters)

Scene: The shore of the Thracian Chersonese in front of a tent housing the captive Trojan women. The time is just before dawn.

(Enter the Ghost of Polydorus.)

GHOST OF POLYDORUS

Back from the pit of the dead, from the somber door
that opens into hell, where no god goes,
I have come,
the ghost of Polydorus,
last son of Cisseus' daughter Hecuba
and Priam, king of Troy.
My father, fearing
that Troy might fall to the assembled arms of Hellas,
had me conveyed in secret out of danger
sending me here to Thrace, to Polymestor,

his friend, who rules this plain of Chersonese
and curbs with harsh power a nation of horsemen.
With me my father secretly sent much gold,
intending that, if Troy should someday fall,
his living sons might be provided for.
Being the youngest, I was chosen, still too small
and slight to carry arms or throw a spear.
As long as Troy's fixed border stones stood proud
and unbreached, so long as our towers held intact
and Hector, my brother, prospered in the fighting,
I flourished like a green shoot under the care
of my father's Thracian friend—doomed as I was.
But when Troy fell and Hector died,
and picks and shovels rooted up our hearth,
and there, by the altar that a god once built,
Priam fell, butchered by Achilles' son,
then my father's friend killed me heartlessly
for the gold and threw my body to the sea,
so that he'd have the gold himself at home.
Here, pounded by the surf, my corpse still lies,
carried up and down on the heaving swell of the sea,
unburied and unmourned.

Disembodied now,

I hover as a wraith over my mother's head,
riding for three long days upon the air,
since she left Troy and came here to Chersonese.
Here on the shore of Thrace, in sullen idleness
beside its ships, the whole Greek army sits
and cannot sail. For Achilles' ghost appeared
above his tomb and stopped the Achaean fleet
as they stood out for sea on the journey home.
He demanded my sister Polyxena as prize,
the blood of the living to sweeten a dead man's grave.
And he shall have her, a prize of honor and a gift
bestowed upon him by his friends. On this day
destiny shall take my sister down to death.

And you, poor mother, you must see two corpses,
your two last children, each one dead this day,
my unhappy sister and me—I shall appear,
so that at last my body can be buried,
washed up on shore at the feet of a slave.
These were the favors I asked of the gods below—
to find my mother and be buried by her hands—
and they have granted my request.
Now I go,
for there I see my aged mother coming,
stumbling from Agamemnon's tent, still shaken
by that dream in which she saw my ghost.

(Enter Hecuba from the tent, accompanied by some Trojan serving women.)

—O Mother,
fallen from a royal palace to a slave's life,
as wretched now as formerly you were blessed!
It must be that some god destroys you now,
making you pay for having once been happy.

(Exit Ghost of Polydorus.)

HECUBA [*chanting*]
O helplessness of age!
Too old, too weak, to stand—
Help me, women of Troy.
Give this slave those hands
you offered to her once
when she was queen of Troy.
Prop me with your arms
and help these useless
stumbling legs to walk.

[*singing*]
O star of morning,
light of Zeus

shining in the night!
What apparition rose,
what shape of terror stalking the darkness?
O goddess Earth,
womb of dreams
with dusky wings!

I repel that dream I dreamed!
that horror that rose in the night, those phantoms of children,°
my son Polydorus in Thrace, Polyxena, my daughter!
Call back that vision of horror!

O gods of the underworld,
preserve my son, save him,
the last surviving anchor of my house,
still dwelling in the snows of Thrace,
still warded by his father's friend!

Disaster I dreamed,
terror on terror!
Never has my heart
so shivered with fear!

O Helenus, I need you now,
interpreter of dreams!
Help me, Cassandra,
help me read my dreams!
I saw a little doe, a dappled doe, torn from between my knees,°
cruelly ripped away, mangled by a wolf with blood-red claw!
And then fresh terror rose:
I saw Achilles' ghost
stalk upon his tomb,
demanding a prize,
one of the wretched women of Troy.

O gods, I implore you,
beat back this dream,
preserve my daughter!

(Enter Chorus of captive Trojan women.)

CHORUS [*chanting*]

I come to you in haste,
Hecuba.
I left the tent
where the lot assigned us.
Slaves, torn from home
when Troy was burnt and sacked
by the conquering Greeks!
I bring you painful news.
I cannot lighten your load.
I bring you worse to bear.
Just now, in full assembly,
the Greek decree came down.
They voted your daughter must die . . .
to be slaughtered alive for Achilles!
The sails had been unfurled,
and the fleet stood out to sea,
when from his tomb Achilles rose,
armor blazing, and held them back,
crying:
"Ho, Argives, where do you sail,
leaving my grave unhonored?"
Waves of argument broke loose,
dividing Greek from Greek.
If one man spoke for death,
another spoke against it.
On your behalf spoke Agamemnon,
lover of your daughter,
poor, mad Cassandra.
Then the two sons of Theseus,
twin shoots of Athens, rose and spoke,
two speeches with one intent—
to crown Achilles' grave
with living blood, asking

if Cassandra's love meant more
than the spear of Achilles.
And so the struggle swayed,
equally poised—
Until he spoke—
that hypocrite with honeyed tongue,
that demagogue Odysseus.
And in the end he won,
asking what any slave was worth
when laid in the balance
with the honor of Achilles.
He wouldn't have the dead
descending down to Hades
telling tales of Greeks,
leaving the field of Troy,
ungrateful to Greeks
who fell for Hellas.
Now Odysseus is coming here
to tear your daughter from your breast
and wrench her from your old arms.
Go to the temples!
Go to the shrines!
Fall at Agamemnon's knees!°
Call on heaven's gods!
Invoke the gods below!
Unless your prayers prevent her death,
unless your pleas can keep her safe,
then you shall see your child,
face downward before the tomb,
as the red blood spreads black
from her gold-jeweled throat.

HECUBA [*singing*]

STROPHE

O grief!

What can I say?
What are the words for loss?
O bitterness of age,
slavery not to be borne,
unendurable!
To whom can I turn?
Childless and homeless,
my husband murdered,
my city stained with fire . . .
Where can I go?
Where shall I find safety?
What god, what power
will help me now?
O women of Troy,
heralds of evil,
bringers of loss,
this news you bring is my sentence of death.
Why should I live? How live in the light
when its goodness is gone,
when all I have is grief?
Bear me up,
poor stumbling feet,
and take me to the tent.
O my child!
Polyxena,
step from the tent!
Come and hear the news
your wretched mother brings,
this news of horror°
that touches your life!

(Enter Polyxena from the tent.)

POLYXENA [*chanting throughout the following interchange with Hecuba, who also chants*]
That terror in your voice!

That cry of fear
flushing me forth
like a bird in terror!

HECUBA
O my child! My baby . . .

POLYXENA
Again that ill-omened cry! Why this evil prelude?

HECUBA
I am afraid for you—

POLYXENA
Tell me the truth now, Mother.
I am afraid, I am afraid.
Why are you groaning?

HECUBA
O my child! My child—

POLYXENA
You must tell me, Mother.

HECUBA
The Greeks,
in full assembly,
have decreed your death,
a living sacrifice
upon Achilles' tomb.

POLYXENA
Oh no, Mother, what are you saying?
Tell me this horrible evil,
tell me, Mother.

HECUBA
I tell you, child, ill-omened news,
the Argives have voted about your fate.

POLYXENA [*now singing*]

ANTISTROPHE

O my poor mother!
How I pity you,
this brokenhearted life
of pain!
What god
could make you suffer so,
impose such pain,
such grief in one poor life?
Alive, at least
I might have shared
your slavery with you,
my unhappy youth
with your miserable age.
But now I die,
and you must see my death—
butchered like a calf,
like a wild mountain beast's young,
ripped from your arms,°
throat cut, and sinking
downward into dark
with the unconsolable dead.
[*now chanting again*]
It is you I pity,°
Mother.
For you I cry.
Not for myself,
not for this life
whose suffering is such
I do not care to live,
but call it happiness to die.

CHORUS LEADER [*speaking*]

Look, Hecuba. Odysseus is coming here
quickly. There must be news.

(Enter Odysseus from the side, attended by several soldiers.)

ODYSSEUS

By now, woman,
I think you know what decision the army has taken
and how we voted.
But let me review the facts.
The Greeks have decreed to sacrifice your daughter
Polyxena at the mound of Achilles' tomb.
The army has delegated me to act as escort.
Achilles' son will supervise the rite
and officiate as priest.
There matters rest.
You understand your position? You must not attempt
to hold your daughter here by force, nor,
I might add, presume to match your strength with mine.
Remember your weakness and accept this tragic loss
as best you can.
Under the circumstances,
the logical course is resignation.

HECUBA

O gods,
it seems a great ordeal of suffering is here,
one full of groans and tears.
Why do I live?
I should have died, I now see, long ago.
But Zeus kept me alive instead, poor wretch,
only to suffer, each time to suffer worse
than all the grief that went before.
Odysseus,
if a slave may make inquiries of the free—
without intent to hurt or give offense—
then let me ask some questions of you now
and hear your answers.

ODYSSEUS

Ask me your questions.
I can spare you the time.

HECUBA

Do you remember once
how you came to Troy, a spy, in beggar's disguise,
smeared with filth, in rags, and blood was streaming
from your brows down to your chin?

ODYSSEUS

I remember
the incident. It left its mark on me.

HECUBA

But Helen penetrated your disguise
and told me who you were? Told me alone?

ODYSSEUS

I stood, I remember, in danger of death.

HECUBA

And how humble you were? How you fell at my knees
and begged for life?

ODYSSEUS

And my hand almost froze on your dress.

HECUBA

And you were at my mercy, my slave then.
Do you remember what you said?

ODYSSEUS

Said?
Anything I could. Anything to live.

HECUBA

And I let you have your life? I let you go?

ODYSSEUS

Because of what you did, I live today.

HECUBA

Then can you say that all these plans of yours
are not contemptible? To take from me
what you confess you took, and in return
do everything you can to do me wrong
and ruin me?
O gods, spare me the sight
of this thankless breed, these politicians
who do not care what harm they do their friends,
providing they can please a crowd!
Tell me,
what cleverness can justify their vote
to kill this girl?
Necessity of fate?
But how? What kind of necessity requires
the shedding of human blood upon a grave,
where custom calls for cattle?
Or is it vengeance
that Achilles' ghost demands, death for his death,
and exacts of her? But what has she to do
with his revenge? Who ever hurt him less
than this poor girl? If death is what he wants,
let Helen die. He went to Troy for her;
for her he died.
Or is it merely looks
that you require, some surpassing beauty in a girl
for this fastidious ghost? Then do not look
for loveliness from us. Look to Helen,
loveliest of lovely women on this earth
by far—lovely Helen, who did him harm
far more than we.
So much by way of answer
to the justice of your case.
Now, Odysseus,
I present my claim for your consideration,

my just demand for payment of your debt
of life.
You admit yourself you took my hand;
you grasped my cheek and begged for life.
But see—

(Hecuba kneels at the feet of Odysseus and takes his hand.)

now I touch you in turn as you touched me.
I kneel before you on the ground and beg
for mercy back:
Let her stay with me.
Let her live.
Surely there are dead enough
without her death. And everything I lost
lives on in her. This one life
redeems the rest. She is my comfort, my Troy,
my staff, my nurse; she guides me on my way.
She is all I have.
And you have power,
Odysseus, greatness and power. But clutch them gently,
use them kindly, and don't suppose, because
you're lucky now, that it will last. It won't.
All greatness goes.
I know. I too was great
but I am nothing now. One day
cut down my greatness and my joy.
But I implore you,
Odysseus, be merciful, take pity on me!
Go to the Greeks. Argue, coax them, convince them
that what they do is wrong. Accuse them of murder!
Tell them we are helpless, we are women,
the same women whom they tore from sanctuary
at the altars. But they pitied us, they spared us then.
Plead with them.
Read them your law of murder. Tell them how

it applies to slave and free without distinction.
But go.
Even if your arguments were weak,
if you faltered or forgot your words, it would not matter.
That prestige you have will guarantee success.
The same speech has a different effect
spoken by a famous man or by a cipher.

CHORUS LEADER
No man could be so callous or so hard of heart
that he could hear your heartbreak and not weep.

ODYSSEUS
Allow me to give you, Hecuba, some good advice,
and don't in anger think me your enemy.

I readily admit how much I owe you,
and in return I stand ready and willing
to honor my debt by saving your life. Indeed,
I have never suggested otherwise.
But note:
I gave my word that when we captured Troy
your daughter should be given to our best soldier
as a prize upon request. That was my promise,
a solemn public commitment which I intend to keep.
Besides, there is a principle at stake
in whose neglect cities have come to grief,
because their keenest, their most exceptional men
received no greater honor than the common run.
And Achilles deserves our honor far more than most,
a great man and a great soldier who died greatly
for his country.
Tell me, what conduct could be worse
than to give your friend a lifetime of honor and respect
but neglect him when he dies?
And what then,

if war should come again and we enlist our citizens
to serve? Would we fight or would we save our skins,
seeing that dead men get no honor?
No:
for my lifetime give me nothing more than what I need;
I ask no more. But as regards my grave,
I hope for honor, since that gratitude
lasts for a lengthy time.
You speak of pity,
but I can talk of pity too. Pity us,
pity our old people, those men and women in Greece
no less miserable than you, the brides and parents
of all those brave young men who found a grave
in the dust of Troy.
Endure; bear your losses,
and if you think me wrong to honor courage
in a man, then call me callous.
But what of you,
barbarians who refuse your dead their rights
and break your faith with friends? And then you wonder
that Hellas should prosper while your countries suffer
the fate they deserve!

CHORUS LEADER

This is what it means
to be a slave: to be abused and bear it,
compelled by violence to suffer wrong.

HECUBA

O my child,
all my prayers are lost, thrown away
on the empty air!
So try your powers now.
Implore him, use every skill that pity has,
every voice. Be like the nightingale,
touch him, move him! Fall at his knees,

beg him for life!
For he has children too
and may pity them in you.

POLYXENA

I see your hand,
Odysseus, hidden in the folds of your robes and your face
averted, lest I try to touch your chin
and beg for life.
Have no fear. You are safe
from me.
I shall not call on Zeus who helps
the helpless.
I shall not beg for life.
No:
I go with you because I must, but most
because I wish to die. If I refuse,
I prove myself a coward, in love with life.
But why should I live?
I had a father once,
king of all Phrygia. And so I started life,
a princess of the blood, nourished on lovely hopes
to be a bride for kings—that suitors would come
competing for my hand, while over the maidens
and women of Troy, I stood acknowledged mistress,
among the girls equal to a goddess,
though bound by death.
And now I am a slave.
It is that name of slave, so ugly, so strange,
that makes me want to die. Or should I live
to be sold to some pitiless new master
for cash? Sister of Hector, sister of princes,
at work in the kitchen, standing by the loom,
and scrubbing the floors, compelled to drag out
endless weary days? And the bride of kings,
forced by some low slave from god knows where

to share his filthy bed?
Never.
With eyes still free, I now renounce the light
and dedicate myself to death.
Odysseus,
lead me off. For I see nothing in this life
to give me hope, and nothing here at all
worth living for.
As for you, Mother,
do nothing, say nothing now to hinder me.
Help me instead; help me to die, now,
before I live disgraced.
I am a novice
to miseries, whose yoke I might endure,
but with such pain that I prefer to die
than go on living badly.

CHORUS LEADER

Noble birth
is a stamp, conspicuous, awesome, among mortals.
And nobility's name grows greater with worthy actions.

HECUBA

I am proud of you, my child, but anguish sticks
in these fine words.
If your Achilles
must have his victim, Odysseus, if you
have any care for your own honor left,
then let her live. Let me take her place
upon the tomb; kill me; be merciless
to me, not her. For I gave birth to Paris
whose arrows brought Achilles down.

ODYSSEUS

The ghost
demanded this girl's blood, not yours,
old woman.

HECUBA

Then let me die with her at least,
and we shall be a double drink of blood
for earth and this demanding ghost below.

ODYSSEUS

Your daughter's death will do. We should not pile
one on another. If only we did not need
this one!

HECUBA

But I must die with her! I must!

ODYSSEUS

Must? A strong word, Hecuba. It was my impression
I was the master here.

HECUBA

I shall stick to her
like ivy to the oak.

ODYSSEUS

Take my advice, Hecuba.
For your own good, do not.

HECUBA

Never, never
will I let her go.

ODYSSEUS

While I, for my part,
refuse to leave her here.

POLYXENA

Mother, listen.
And you, Odysseus, be gentle with a mother's love.
She has reasons for her anger.
Poor Mother,
do not struggle with those stronger than you.
Is this what you want—to be thrown down in the dust,

this poor old body torn away from me,
humiliated by younger and stronger arms?
They will do it. No, this is not for you.
O Mother, Mother,
give me your hand,
and put your cheek to mine for one last time
and then no more. For the last, last time
I look upon this gleaming circle of the sun
and speak the last words I shall ever say.
O Mother, Mother,
now I go below!

HECUBA

Leaving me to live, a slave in the light!°

POLYXENA

Unmarried to my death, no wedding songs for me!

HECUBA

Pity for you, and wretchedness for me!

POLYXENA

To lie in the dark in Hades, far from you!

HECUBA

O gods, where can I go? Where shall I die?

POLYXENA

I was born to freedom and I die a slave.

HECUBA

Fifty children I once had, and all are dead.

POLYXENA

What message shall I take to Hector and old Priam?

HECUBA

Tell them this: I am the queen of sorrow.

POLYXENA

O sweet breasts that nourished me!

HECUBA

So wrong, so wrong! So young to die!

POLYXENA

Farewell, Cassandra! Mother, farewell!

HECUBA

Let others fare well. I never shall.

POLYXENA

Goodbye, Polydorus, my brother in Thrace!

HECUBA

If he lives at all—for all I have is loss.

POLYXENA

He lives. He will close your dying eyes.

HECUBA

I have died of sorrow while I was still alive.

POLYXENA

Shroud my head, Odysseus, and lead me out.
Even before I die, my cries have broken
my mother's heart, and she has broken mine.
O light of day!
I still can cry the light
in that little space of life I have to live
before I die upon Achilles' tomb!

(Exit Odysseus and Polyxena to the side.)

HECUBA

I am faint—my legs give way beneath me—
Polyxena!
Touch your mother, give me your hand,
reach me! Do not leave me childless!
My friends,
I've been destroyed. If only I could see
Helen of Sparta, sister of Zeus' sons,

destroyed like me. For she with her fair eyes
made ashes of the happiness of Troy!

CHORUS [*singing*]

STROPHE A

O wind of ocean,
wind that blows on the sea
and drives the scudding ships,
where are you blowing me?
Where shall I be slave?
Where is there home for me?
There in distant Doris,
or in Phthia far away
where men say Apidanus runs,
father of waters, river whose lovely flowing
fattens the fields?

ANTISTROPHE A

Or there in the islands?
The salt sea churning, borne on by oars,
to days of mourning in the house,
there where the primal palm
and the bay broke out their leaves
for lovely Leto
in honor of her son?
There shall I sing
with the maidens of Delos,
praising Artemis'
bow and fillets of gold?

STROPHE B

Or in the city of Pallas,
in Athens, shall I yoke
the horses on the goddess' robe,
stitching cloth of saffron
with threads of every color,
sewing the Titans there,

who were killed by stabbing fire,
the thunderbolts of Zeus?

ANTISTROPHE B

O my children!
O my forefathers!
O city, ruined land,
ashes and smoke, wasted
by the spear of the Argives!
I live, but live a slave,
forced to a foreign land,
torn westward out of Asia,
exchanging the chambers of death
for a home in Europe!

(Enter Talthybius from the side.)

TALTHYBIUS

Women of Troy, where can I find Hecuba,
your onetime queen?

CHORUS LEADER

There she lies, Talthybius,
in the dust at your feet, her head buried in her robes.

TALTHYBIUS

O Zeus, what can I say?
That you look on mankind
and care?
Or do we, holding that the gods exist,
deceive ourselves with unsubstantial lies
while chance controls the world?
Is this the queen
of Troy once rich in gold? Is this the wife
of Priam the great?
And now, childless, old,
enslaved, her home and city wrecked by war,
she lies there on the ground, her wretched head
fouled in the dust.

Oh horror! I am old,
but I would rather die than sink as low
as this poor woman has fallen now.
Rise,
unhappy lady. Lift your body up,
and raise your white-haired head.

HECUBA

Who are you
who will not let me lie? Who disturbs
my wretchedness? Why?

TALTHYBIUS

I am Talthybius,
servant of the Greeks, lady. I bring you a message
from Agamemnon.

HECUBA

Have the Greeks decreed my death?
Tell me that, and you are welcome, dearest man.
No other news could please me better now.
Let's go in haste. You lead the way, old man.

TALTHYBIUS

No, not that.
I come on behalf of the army and the sons of Atreus
to bid you bury your daughter. She is dead.

HECUBA

Is that your news, herald?
So I cannot die?
You came to tell me this?
O gods, my child!
My poor child! Torn from my arms! Dead!
Dead. Without you, I now am childless.
So how did you all put her to death? With honor
and respect, or did you kill her savagely,
as an enemy? Tell me, old man. Let me hear it all,
no matter how it hurts.

TALTHYBIUS

There is a cost
in telling too, a double price of tears,
for I was crying when your daughter died,
and I will cry again while telling you,
lady. But listen.
The whole army of the Greeks
was present for your daughter's sacrifice,
and Achilles' son took Polyxena's hand
and led her up the tomb. I stood nearby;
with them, a troop of soldiers purposely appointed
to prevent her struggles.
Then Achilles' son
lifted a golden beaker to pour the offering
of wine to his dead father and nodded to me
to call for silence.
"Quiet, Achaeans!" I shouted,
"Silence in the ranks! Keep quiet!" A hush
fell upon the army and he began to pray:
"Father Achilles, Peleus' son, receive
this offering I pour to summon your spirit up.
Rise and drink this gift we give to you,
this virgin's dark blood. Be gracious to us:
set free our ships and loose our mooring ropes.
Grant to us all our day of coming home,
grant us all to come home safe from Troy!"
So he prayed, and the army with him.
Then,
grasping the hilt of his gilded sword, he drew it
from the sheath, and nodded to the chosen youths
to seize her. But she spoke first:
"Wait, you Greeks
who sacked my city! Of my own free will I die.
Let no man touch me. I offer my throat
bravely to the sword. But by the gods,
let me be free for now. Let me die free.

I am of royal blood, and I scorn to be called
a slave among the dead."
"Yes!" the army roared,
and Agamemnon told the young men to let her go.
And they, when they had heard the final decree°
of the man with highest authority, let go.
When she heard the rulers' words she grasped her robes
and ripped them open from the shoulder down
as far as the waist, exposing her naked breasts,
bare and lovely like a sculptured goddess.
Then she sank, kneeling on the ground, and gave
this most heroic speech:
"Strike, captain.
Here is my breast. Will you stab me there?
Or in the neck? Here is my throat, ready
for your blow."
Torn between pity and duty,
Achilles' son stood hesitating, and then
slashed her throat with the edge of his sword. The blood
gushed out, and she fell, dying, to the ground,
but even as she dropped, managed to fall somehow
with grace, modestly hiding what should be hidden
from men's eyes.
The execution finished,
the soldiers set to work. Some scattered leaves
upon her corpse, while others brought big logs
of pine and heaped her pyre. Those who shirked
found themselves abused by the rest.
"You loafers,"
they shouted, "how can you stand there empty-handed,
doing nothing? Where's your present for the girl?
When did you ever see greater courage
than that?"
And now you know it all.
For my part,
having seen your daughter die, I count you

of all women the one most blessed in her children
and also the unhappiest.

CHORUS LEADER

Blow after blow
disaster drops from heaven; suffering shakes
my city and the house of Priam.

HECUBA

O my child,
how shall I deal with this thronging crowd of blows,
these sufferings, each with its petition, clamoring
for attention? If I lay my hand on one,
another shoulders in, and then a third
comes on, distracting, each fresh sorrow
breeding new successors in its turn.
But now,
although I can't forget your death, can't stop
crying—
yet a kind of comfort comes in knowing
how nobly you died.
And yet how strange it seems.
Even worthless ground, given a gentle push
from heaven, will harvest well, while fertile soil,
starved of what it needs, bears badly.
But human nature never seems to change;
ignoble stays itself, bad to the end;
and nobility good, its nature uncorrupted
by any shock or blow, always the same,
enduring excellence.
Is it in our blood°
or something we acquire? But goodness can be taught,
and any man who knows what goodness is
knows evil too, because he judges
from the good.
But all this is the rambling nonsense
of despair.

Talthybius, go to the Greeks
and tell them this from me: that not a hand
is to be laid on my child; make them keep
the crowd away.
For in armies the size of this,
men are prone to violence, sailors undisciplined
worse than a fire, while the man who stands apart
is called a coward.

(Exit Talthybius to the side.)

—Take your pitcher, old servant,
fill it with water from the sea and then return.
I must give my daughter's body its last bath
before her burial, this wedding which is death.
For she marries Achilles, and I must bathe the bride
and lay her out—not as she deserves, but as well
as I can.
But how? I've nothing precious left.
What then?
I'll gather from my women in the tent
whatever poor trinkets they managed to pilfer
from their own homes.

(Exit Handmaid to the side.)

Where is greatness gone?
Where is it now, that stately house, the home
that was so happy once? King Priam,
blessed with children once, in your pride of wealth?
And what am I of all I used to be,
mother of sons, mother of princes?
Gone,
all gone, and nothing left.
Now who
will boast, be proud, or plume his confidence—
the rich man in his insolence of wealth,
the public man's conceit of office or success?

For we are nothing; our ambition, greatness, pride,
all vanity.
That man is happiest
who lives from day to day and asks no more,
garnering no evil in his simple life.

(Exit Hecuba into the tent.)

CHORUS [*singing*]

STROPHE

That morning was my fate,
that hour doom was done,
when Paris felled the tree
that grew on Ida's height
and made a ship for sea
and sailed to Helen's bed—
loveliest of women
the golden sun has seen.

ANTISTROPHE

Grief, and worse than grief,
necessity surrounds us.
One man's folly made
a doom shared by all,
ruin over Simois.
Paris sat as judge
upon three goddesses.
His verdict was war.

EPODE

War, slaughter, and the ruin of my house,
while in her house the Spartan girl mourns too,
grieving by the wide Eurotas,
and mothers mourn for their sons,
and tear out their snowy hair
and dredge their cheeks with bloody nails.

(Enter the Handmaid from the side.)

HANDMAID

Where is the queen, women?
Where is Hecuba
whose sufferings outstrip all rival runners?
No one shall take that crown away.

CHORUS LEADER

Speak.
What new sorrow do you bring her? Will all this news
of anguish never sleep?

(Enter other women, carrying on a bier a shrouded corpse.)

HANDMAID

This is the grief
I bring to Hecuba. Gentle words are hard
to find: the burden I bring is disaster.

(Enter Hecuba from the tent.)

CHORUS LEADER

Look: here she's coming now from out the tent,
she's just in time to hear your news.

HANDMAID

My queen,
more wretched, more miserable than I can say.
Now you live no more, the light is gone!
No child, no husband, no city—utterly ruined!

HECUBA

This is mockery, not news. I know it all.
But why have you brought Polyxena's body here?
I heard the Greeks were busied with her funeral.

HANDMAID

Poor woman, she thinks it is Polyxena.
She does not know the worst.

HECUBA

O gods, no!
Not my poor mad daughter, Cassandra?

HANDMAID

Cassandra is alive. Mourn for this dead boy.

(She strips the shroud from the corpse, revealing the dead Polydorus.)

Look at this corpse that I uncover now,
this unexpected horror.

HECUBA

It is my son!
Polydorus, warded by my friend in Thrace!
No!
O gods in heaven, let me die!
[*singing; the Handmaid and the Chorus Leader speak in reply*]
O my son, my son,
now the awful dirge begins,
the fiend, the fury,
singing, wailing in me now,
shrieking madness!

HANDMAID

So now, poor woman, you've seen your child is dead?

HECUBA

Horror too sudden to be believed,
unbelievable loss,
blow after blow!
And this is all my life:
the mourning endless,
the anguish unending.

CHORUS LEADER

Dreadful, poor woman, the evils that we suffer.

HECUBA

O my son, my child,

how were you killed?
What fate, what hand
could take your life?

HANDMAID

I do not know. I found him on the shore.

HECUBA

Drowned, his body washed on the sand?
Or was he murdered?

HANDMAID

The surf had washed his body up.

HECUBA

O gods, my dream!
I see it now,
those black wings beating the dark,
its message has not missed me,
you live no longer in Zeus' light!

CHORUS LEADER

Who murdered him? Did your dream show you that?

HECUBA

Who but my friend, horseman in Thrace,
where his father hid him away from harm?

CHORUS LEADER

Murdered? Murdered by a friend? Killed for gold?

HECUBA

Unspeakable, unimaginable crime,
unbearable!
Where is friendship now?
O fiend, monster, so pitiless,
to mangle him so, to hack
his sweet flesh with the sword!

CHORUS LEADER

Unhappy Hecuba, most miserable of mortals

upon this earth, how heavily some god
falls on you.
—But look: I see your master,
Agamemnon, coming here. So we'll be silent.

(Enter Agamemnon from the side with attendants.)

AGAMEMNON

Why this delay of yours, Hecuba,
in burying your daughter? I received your message
from Talthybius that none of our men should touch her,
and I gave strict orders to that effect.
Hence I found your delay all the more surprising
and came to fetch you myself. In any case,
I can report that matters there are well in hand
and proceeding nicely—if a word like "nicely"
has any meaning in this connection.

(He sees the corpse of Polydorus.)

Here,
what's that Trojan corpse beside the tents?
I can see from his clothes that he's not a Greek.

(Hecuba turns away from him.)

HECUBA *(Aside.)*

Poor Hecuba—it's I that I mean now,
saying "you"—what shall I do?
Throw myself
at his knees and beg for mercy or hold my tongue
and suffer in silence?

AGAMEMNON

Why do you turn away
in silence? And what's the meaning of these tears?
What happened here? Who is this man?

HECUBA (*Aside.*)

But suppose he treats me like an enemy slave,
and pushes me away? I could not bear it.

AGAMEMNON

I am not a prophet, Hecuba. Unless you speak,
you make it quite impossible for me to help you.

HECUBA (*Aside.*)

And yet I could be wrong. Am I imagining?
He may mean well.

AGAMEMNON

If you have nothing to say,
Hecuba, very well. I have no wish to hear.

HECUBA (*Aside.*)

But without his help I lose my only chance
of revenging my children. So why should I hesitate?
Win or lose, he is my only hope.

(*She turns to Agamemnon and falls at his knees.*)

Agamemnon, I implore you, I beg you
by your chin, your knees, by this conquering hand, help me!

AGAMEMNON

What can I do to help you, Hecuba? Your freedom
is yours for the asking.

HECUBA

No, not freedom.
Revenge. Only give me my revenge
and I'll gladly stay a slave the rest of my life.

AGAMEMNON

Well, what's the help you're asking me for?

HECUBA

My lord,

not the revenge you think, not that at all.
Do you see this body here for which I mourn?

AGAMEMNON

I see him—but I don't see what this means.

HECUBA

This was my son. I gave him birth.

AGAMEMNON

Which son,

poor woman?

HECUBA

Not one of Priam's sons who died

in Troy.

AGAMEMNON

You mean you had another son?

HECUBA

Another son, in vain. This was he.

AGAMEMNON

But where was he living when Troy was taken?

HECUBA

His father sent him away to save his life.

AGAMEMNON

This was the only son he sent away?
Where did he send him?

HECUBA

Here. To this country

where his body was found.

AGAMEMNON

He sent him to Polymestor,

the king of Thrace?

HECUBA

And with his son he also sent
a sum of fatal gold.

AGAMEMNON

But how did he die? Who killed him?

HECUBA

Who else
could it have been? His host, our Thracian friend.

AGAMEMNON

Then his motive, you think, was the gold?

HECUBA

Yes.
The instant he heard that Troy had fallen, he killed.

AGAMEMNON

But where was the body found? Who brought him here?

HECUBA

This woman servant here. She found his body
lying on the beach.

AGAMEMNON

What was she doing there?
Searching for him?

HECUBA

No. She went for water
for Polyxena's burial.

AGAMEMNON

He must have killed him first,
then thrown his body in the sea.

HECUBA

Hacked him, tossed him
to the pounding surf.

AGAMEMNON

I pity you, Hecuba.
Your suffering has no end.

HECUBA

I died
long ago. Nothing can touch me now.

AGAMEMNON

What woman on this earth was ever cursed
like this?

HECUBA

There is none but goddess Fortune
herself.
But let me tell you why I kneel
at your feet. And if my sufferings seem just,
then I must be content. But if otherwise,
give me my revenge on that treacherous friend
who flouted every god in heaven and in hell
to do this impious murder.
At our table°
he was our frequent guest; was counted first
among our friends, respected, honored by me,
receiving every kindness that a man could meet—
and then, in cold deliberation, killed
my son.
Murder may have its reasons, its motives,
but he even refused my son a grave and threw him
to the sea, unburied!
I am a slave, I know,
and slaves are weak. But the gods are strong, and over them
there stands the law that governs all. It is
by virtue of this law that we believe
the gods exist, and by this law we live,
distinguishing good from evil.

Apply that law
now. For if you flout it, so that those
who murder their own guests or defy the gods
go unpunished, then human justice withers,
corrupted at its source.
Honor my request,
Agamemnon.
Punish this murder.
Pity me.
Be like a painter. Stand back, see me
in perspective,
see me whole, observe
my wretchedness—
once a queen, and now
a slave; blessed with children, happy once,
now old, no children, no city, utterly alone,
unhappiest of mortals . . .

(Agamemnon turns away.)

O no! You turn away—
what can I do? My only hope is lost.
O this helplessness!
Why, why
do we make so much of knowledge, struggle so hard
to get some skill, quite rightly, at many things,
but persuasion, the only art whose power
is absolute, worth any price we pay,
the sole ruler over human minds, by which
we persuade others and gain what we want—persuasion
we totally neglect. And so we fail;
we lose our hopes.
I have seen my children die,
and bound to shame I walk this homeless earth,
a slave, and see the smoke that leaps up
over Troy.

It may be futile now
to urge the claims of love, but let me urge them
anyway. At your side sleeps my daughter
Cassandra, once the priestess of Apollo.
What will you give, my lord, for those nights of love?
What thanks for all her tenderness in bed
does she receive from you, and I, in turn,
for her?°
Look now at this dead boy,
Cassandra's brother. Help him, and you help
your brother-in-law. Revenge him.
One word more.
If by some magic, some gift of the gods,
I could become all speech—tongues in my arms,
hands that talked, voices from my hair and feet—
then, all together, I'd fall and touch your knees,
crying, begging, imploring with a thousand tongues—
O master, greatest light of Hellas, hear me,
help an old woman, though she's worth nothing, avenge her!
You must do your duty as a man of honor:
see justice done. Punish the murderer.

CHORUS LEADER

How strange in their reversals are our lives!
The laws of harsh necessity° decide,
joining enemies in common cause
and alienating friends.

AGAMEMNON

I pity you deeply,
Hecuba, for the terrible death of this poor boy.
And I am moved by your fortunes and suppliant hand.
So far as justice is concerned, the gods know well,
nothing would please me more than to bring
this murderer to book.
But my position
here is delicate. If I give you your revenge,

the army is sure to charge that I connived
at the death of the king of Thrace because of my love
for Cassandra. This is my dilemma. The army
thinks of Polymestor as its friend,
this boy as its enemy—if to me° he's precious,
that's irrelevant and no matter to the Greeks.
Put yourself in my position.
Believe me,
Hecuba, I should like to act on your behalf
and would come instantly to your defense.
But if the army complains, then I must
be slow.

HECUBA

Then no man on earth is truly free.
All are slaves of money or necessity.
Or public opinion or fear of prosecution
prevents each one from doing what he thinks
is right.
But since your fears make you defer
to the mob, let me, a slave, set you free
from what you fear.
Be my confidant,
the silent partner of my plot to kill my son's
murderer. Give me your passive support.
Then if some uproar breaks out or the Greeks
attempt a rescue, obstruct them covertly
without appearing to act for me.
For the rest,
have no fear. I shall manage.

AGAMEMNON

How?
Poison? Or do you think your agèd hand
could lift a sword and kill? Who would help you?
On whom could you count?

HECUBA

Remember: Trojan women
are hidden in these tents.

AGAMEMNON

You mean our prisoners?

HECUBA

They will help me get revenge.

AGAMEMNON

But women?
Women overpower men?

HECUBA

There's dreadful power
in numbers, when they are combined with cunning.

AGAMEMNON

True,
though I admit to being skeptical of women
in a matter like this.

HECUBA

Why?

Women killed
Aegyptus' sons. Women emptied Lemnos
of its males: they murdered every one. And so
it shall be here. Let's bandy no more words,
and let this woman here have your safe-conduct
through the army.

(Agamemnon nods. Hecuba turns to the Handmaid.)

Go to our Thracian friend
and give him this message:
"Hecuba, once queen of Troy,
summons you on business that concerns you both
and requests you bring your sons. They also share
in what she has to say."

(Exit Handmaid with one or more of Agamemnon's attendants to the side.)

One more favor,
Agamemnon.
Defer my daughter's funeral
until my son's corpse can be placed beside her
on the pyre. Let them burn together,
brother and sister joined in a single flame,
their mother's double grief.

AGAMEMNON

As you wish.
If we could sail, I could not grant this. But now,
until the god sends us a favoring wind,
we must ride at anchor here and wait to sail.
May things turn out well! The common interests
of states and individuals alike demand
that good men prosper and evil men be punished.

(Exit Agamemnon to the side, followed by attendants. Exit Hecuba and her women into the tent with the body of Polydorus.)

CHORUS [*singing*]

STROPHE A

O Ilium! O my country,
whose name men speak no more
among unfallen cities!
So dense a cloud of Greeks
came, spear on spear, destroying!
Your crown of towers shorn away,
and everywhere the staining smoke,
most pitiful. O Ilium,
whose streets I shall not walk again!

ANTISTROPHE A

At midnight came my doom,
midnight when the feast is done

and sleep falls sweetly on the eyes.
The songs and sacrifice,
the dances, all were done.
My husband lay asleep,
his spear upon the wall,
on Ilium's peak,
no longer seeing the ships
massed on Ilium's shore.

STROPHE B

I was setting my hair
in the soft folds of the net,
gazing at the endless light
deep in the golden mirror,
preparing myself for bed,
when tumult broke the air
and shouts and cries
shattered the empty streets—
"Onward, onward, you Greeks!
Sack the city of Troy
and see your homes once more!"

ANTISTROPHE B

Dressed only in one gown
like a girl of Sparta,
I left the bed of love
and prayed to Artemis.
But the answer was, "No."
I saw my husband lying dead,
and they took me away to the sea.
Backward I looked at Troy,
as the ship sped on
and Ilium slipped away,
and I was dumb with grief.

EPODE

A curse on Helen,
sister of the sons of Zeus,

and my curse on him,
disastrous Paris,
whose wedding wasted my Troy
and banished me from my home!
No marriage but a curse, the curse of some demon!
Let the salty sea
never bring her home!
Let there be no return
for Helen of Troy!

(Enter Polymestor from the side, followed by his two young sons, the Handmaid, and several attendants. Hecuba keeps her eyes fixed on the ground.)

POLYMESTOR

Dearest Hecuba, wife of my dear friend,
poor unhappy Priam!°
How I pity you,
you and your ruined Troy. And now this latest blow,
your daughter's death . . .
What can we take on trust
in this uncertain life? Happiness, greatness,
fame—nothing is secure, nothing keeps.
The inconsistent gods make chaos of our lives,
pitching us about with such savagery of change
that we, out of our anguish and uncertainty,
may turn to them.
But how does my sorrow help?
Your loss remains.
But perhaps you are angry with me, Hecuba,
for not coming to you earlier. If so, forgive me.
It just so happened that I was inland, in the middle
of Thrace, at the time when you arrived. In fact,
I was on the point of coming here myself
when your servant arrived and gave me your message.
Needless to say, I lost no time.

HECUBA

Polymestor,
I am so embarrassed by the state in which you see me,
fallen so low since when you saw me last,
I cannot look you in the face.
Forgive it,
and do not think me rude, Polymestor.
In any case, habit and custom excuse me,°
forbidding that a woman look directly at a man.

POLYMESTOR

I quite understand.
Now, how can I help you?
You sent for me on some business, I believe?

HECUBA

I have a matter to discuss with you and your sons.
But privately, if possible.
Could you ask your men
to withdraw?

POLYMESTOR *(To his attendants.)*

You may leave. There is no danger here.
This woman is my friend and the army of the Greeks
is well disposed.

(Exit his attendants to the side.)

Now, Hecuba, to business.
How can I, your prosperous friend, help you now
in your time of troubles? I am ready.

HECUBA

First
one question. How's my son Polydorus, your ward?
Is he alive?
Anything else can wait.

POLYMESTOR

Alive and well. In this respect at least,
you may put your mind at rest.

HECUBA

My dearest friend,
how like you your kindness is!

POLYMESTOR

What else
would give you comfort?

HECUBA

Does he still remember his mother?

POLYMESTOR

So much that he wanted to run away
and visit you in secret.

HECUBA

And the gold from Troy?
Is it safe?

POLYMESTOR

Quite safe. Locked in my palace
under strong guard.

HECUBA

Guard it well, my friend.
Do not let it tempt you.

POLYMESTOR

Have no fears.
I hope that what I have myself will stand
me in good stead.

HECUBA

Do you know why I sent for you
and your sons?

POLYMESTOR

Not yet. We are waiting to hear.

HECUBA

You are my friend, a friend for whom I feel
no less love than you have shown to me.
And my business concerns . . .

POLYMESTOR

Yes? Yes? Go on.

HECUBA

. . . the ancient vaults, the gold of Priam's house.

POLYMESTOR

I am to pass this information to your son?

HECUBA

In person. I know you for a man of honor.

POLYMESTOR

But why did you ask that my sons be present?

HECUBA

I thought they should know. Something, for instance,
might happen to you.

POLYMESTOR

A prudent precaution.
I quite agree.

HECUBA

Do you know where Athena's temple
once stood in Troy?

POLYMESTOR

The gold is there?
Is there a marker?

HECUBA

A black rock jutting up
above the ground.

POLYMESTOR

Is that all?

HECUBA

No:
my money. I smuggled some money away from Troy.
Could you keep it for me?

POLYMESTOR

You have it on you?
Where is it hidden?

HECUBA

There, inside the tent,
beneath a heap of spoils.

POLYMESTOR

Inside the tent?
Here, in the Greek camp?

HECUBA

The women's quarters
are separate from the main camp.

POLYMESTOR

Is it safe?
Are there men around?

HECUBA

No Greeks; only women.
But come inside. We have no time to lose.
Quick.
The Greek army is waiting and eager
to raise their anchors and sail for home.
Then,
when our business here is done, you may go
and take your children where you left my son.

(Exit Polymestor and his sons, accompanied by Hecuba, into the tent.)

CHORUS LEADER

Death is life's debt. Perhaps now yours falls due.

CHORUS [*singing*]

As though you stumbled in the surf
hurled from high ambition down
trapped, thrashing with terror
in the swirling tow
and the water
closing overhead
until
you drown.
And now you know:
Those who take a life—
repay it with their own.
Justice and the gods
exact the loan at last.
Your hopes for this road misled you.
You took the final turn
where the bitter road veers off
and runs downhill
to death!
Hands which never held a sword
shall wrench your twisted life away!

(Screams and commotion are heard from inside the tent.)

POLYMESTOR *(From within.)*

Blind! Blind!
O light!
Light of my eyes!

CHORUS LEADER

That scream of anguish! Did you hear, my friends?

POLYMESTOR *(From within.)*

Help!
Look out, children!

Murder!

Run! Murder!

CHORUS LEADER

New murder, fresh horror in the tent!

POLYMESTOR *(From within.)*

Run! Will you run?
But I'll get you yet!
I'll batter down this tent with my bare fists!
See there, a heavy fist has launched its blow!°

CHORUS LEADER

What should we do?
Break down the door?
Hurry!
Hecuba needs our help!

(Enter Hecuba from the tent.)

HECUBA

Pound away!
Go on, batter down the door!
Nothing can ever give you back the light
of your eyes.
Never shall you see your sons
alive again. For I have killed them both!

CHORUS LEADER

Have you done it? Have you felled your Thracian host
and rule him now? Have you done this thing you say?

HECUBA

Be patient a moment, and then see for yourself.
Watch him as he stumbles and staggers out of the tent—
stone-blind.
See the bodies of his two sons,
killed by my women and me.
His debt is paid

and I have my revenge.
But hush: here he comes,
raging from the tent. Let me keep out of his reach.
In his Thracian fury he will stop at nothing.

(Enter Polymestor blinded from the tent on all fours. His sons' bodies are visible in the doorway of the tent.)

POLYMESTOR [*singing*]
Where?
Where shall I run?
Where shall I stop?
Where?
Like a raging beast I go,
running on all fours
on my hands on the track!
Where?
Where?
Here?
Where?
Where can I pounce
on those murderous hags of Troy?
Where are you, women?
Where are they hiding,
those bitches of Troy?

O god of the sun,
heal these bleeding eyes!
Give me back the light of my eyes!
Shh.
The sound of footsteps.
But where?
Where can I leap?
To gorge their blood,
to rip the living flesh,
feed like a starving beast,

blood for blood, outrage for outrage!
No, no.
Where am I running now?
My children abandoned,
for Bacchants of hell to claw,
for savage bitches to gorge,
their mangled bodies thrown
pitilessly on the hill!
But where?
Where shall I run?
Where can I stand at bay?
Run, run, run,
gather robes and run!
Let me run for my lair,
race like a ship,
sails furled, for the shore!
I'll run for my lair
and stand at bay
where my children lie!

CHORUS LEADER

Tormented man! Tortured past enduring.
You suffer now as you made others suffer.°

POLYMESTOR [*singing*]

Help me, you men of Thrace!
Help!
Soldiers, horsemen,
help! Come with spears!
Achaeans, help! Help me,
sons of Atreus!
Help!
Help!
Hear me, help me, help!
Where are you?
Help me!

Women have destroyed me.
Dreadful sufferings!
Butchery! Horror!
Help me!
Help!
Where can I go?
Where can I run?
You gods in heaven,
give me wings to fly!
Let me leap to heaven
where the vaulted stars,
Sirius and Orion,
flare out their fire,
or plunge to Hades
on the blackened flood!

CHORUS LEADER

Who could reproach this man for wanting to die?
Death is what men want when the anguish of living
is more than they can bear.

(Enter Agamemnon from the side, attended by soldiers.)

AGAMEMNON

Shouting and screams
of terror brought me here. Ringing Echo,
born of the mountain crags, resounded the cries
throughout the camp. Unless we knew for a fact
that Troy had fallen to our arms, this uproar
could have caused no little terror or disturbance.

POLYMESTOR

That voice! I know it.
My friend, Agamemnon!
Look, look at me now!

AGAMEMNON

Oh. Awful sight!
Poor Polymestor! Those blind bleeding eyes,

those dead children . . . Who did this, Polymestor?
Whoever it was must have hated you and your sons
with savage anger.

POLYMESTOR

Hecuba. She did it,
she and the other women. They destroyed me,
they worse than destroyed me.

AGAMEMNON

You, Hecuba?
Do you admit this hideous, inhuman crime?
Is this atrocity your work?

POLYMESTOR

Hecuba?
Is she near?
Where? Tell me where she is,
and I'll claw her to pieces with these bare hands!

AGAMEMNON

What? Have you lost your mind?

POLYMESTOR

For the gods' sake,
let me at her! Let me rip her limb from limb!

AGAMEMNON

Stop.
No more of this barbarian savagery now.
Each of you will give his version of the case
and I shall try to judge you both impartially.

POLYMESTOR

Then listen, Agamemnon.
Hecuba had a son
called Polydorus, her youngest. His father Priam,
apprehensive that Troy would one day be taken,
sent the boy to me to be raised in my own house.

I killed him, and I admit it.
My action, however,
was dictated, as you shall see, by a policy
of wise precaution.
My primary motive was fear,
fear that if this boy, your enemy, survived,
he might someday found a second and resurgent Troy.
Further, when the Greeks heard that Priam's son
was still alive, I feared that they would raise
a second expedition against this new Troy,
in which case these fertile plains of Thrace
would once again be ravaged by war; once again
Troy and her troubles would work her neighbors harm,
as they have done just now.
Hecuba, however,
somehow hearing that her son was dead,
lured me here on the pretext of revealing
the secret hiding place of Priam's gold
in Troy. Then, alleging that we might be overheard,
she led my sons and me, all unattended,
into the tent.
Surrounded by Trojan women
on every side, I sat down on a couch.
The atmosphere seemed one of friendliness.
The women fingered my robes, then lifted the cloth
to inspect it better under the light, exclaiming
over the quality of our Thracian weaving.
Still others stood admiring my two lances
and before I knew it I was stripped of all
my weaponry.
Meanwhile the young mothers
were fussing over my children, jouncing them in their arms
with hugs and kisses and passing them from hand to hand
until they were out of reach.
Then, incredibly,
out of that scene of domestic peace,

they suddenly pulled daggers from their robes
and butchered both my sons, while troops of women
rushed to tackle me, seizing my arms and legs
and holding me down. I tried to leap up
but they caught me by the hair and pulled me down.
I fought to free my arms, but I was swamped
beneath a flood of women. I could not move.
And then they crowned their hideous work with worse,
the most inhuman brutal crime of all.
They took their brooches and stabbed my hapless eyes
till they poured out blood! Then they ran for cover,
scattering through the tent. I leaped to my feet,
like a wounded animal chasing a pack of hounds,
tracking along every wall, like a hunter
beating and striking everywhere.
This is my reward, Agamemnon,
for my efforts in disposing of your enemy.
One word more.
On behalf of all those dead
who learned their hatred of women long ago,
for those who hate them now, for those unborn
who shall live to hate them yet, I now declare
my firm conviction:
neither earth nor ocean
produces a creature as savage and as monstrous
as woman. Any man who has ever met one
will know that this is true.

CHORUS LEADER

Do not presume,
Polymestor, whatever your provocation,
to include all women in this sweeping curse
without distinction.°

HECUBA

The clear actions of a man,
Agamemnon, should speak louder than any words.

Good words should get their goodness from our lives;
the evil that we do should show in speech
and never make injustice sound attractive.
Some men, I know, make a science of such persuasion,
but in the end their speciousness will show.
The impostors are punished; not one escapes
his downfall.
So much by way of beginning.
Now for him.

(To Polymestor.)

You claim you killed my son
on behalf of Agamemnon, and to spare
the Greeks the horrors of a second war.
You liar!
First, what possible friendship could there be
between civilized Greeks and barbarians
like you?
Clearly none.
Then why this zeal
to serve their cause?
Are you related to them?
Or would you be by marriage?
Then what's your motive?
Fear, you say, that they would sail for Troy
and ravage the harvest of your land again.
Who could believe that preposterous lie?
No,
if you'd speak the truth, it was gold and your greed
that killed my son.
For tell me: why, when Troy
still flourished and its ramparts ringed the city,
when Priam was alive and Hector had his day—
why, if you wanted to be Agamemnon's friend,
did you not then kill my son or hand him over
alive to the Greeks? It would have been so easy—

you were keeping and raising him in your house.
But no.
You waited, biding your time, until our sun
had set, and the smoke announced the sack of Troy.
Then you moved, killing your guest and friend
who sat at your hearth.
And what of this,
which shows your crime for what it was?
Why,
if you loved the Greeks as much as you assert,
did you miss your chance to present them with the gold—
that gold you claim does not belong to you
but to Agamemnon? For they were desperate then,
long years away from home.
But no. Even now
you cannot bear the thought of giving up
the gold, but hoard it for yourself at home.
Another point.
If you had done your duty
by my son, raised him and kept him safe,
men would honor and respect you as a noble friend.
For real friendship is shown in times of trouble;
prosperity has friends galore.
And then,
if someday you had stood in need of help
and if my son had prospered he'd have been
a mighty treasury for you. Instead,
you've killed your friend, your gold is worthless now,
your sons are dead, and you are as you are.

(To Agamemnon.)

Agamemnon, this is what I say to you:
if you assist this man, you prove yourself
unjust.
This is a man who betrayed his trust,
who killed against the laws of man and god,

faithless, evil, corrupt.
Assist him now
and we shall say the same is true of you.
But you are my master: I criticize no further.

CHORUS LEADER

Ah, true it is: for mortals, a good cause
will always find good arguments to back it.

AGAMEMNON

It does not give me any satisfaction
to sit as judge on the miseries of others.
But I should cut a sorry figure in the world
if I took on this case and then refused
to give a verdict.
Know then, Polymestor,
I find you guilty of murder as charged.
You murdered your ward, killed him in cold blood,
and not, as you assert, for the Greeks or me,
but out of simple greed, to get his gold.
You then construed the facts to fit your case.
Perhaps you think it but a trifling matter
to kill a guest.
Well, we Greeks call it murder.
How, therefore, could I acquit you now
without incurring blame among men?
I could not.
You committed a brutal crime; therefore accept
the consequences of your act.

POLYMESTOR

Oh no!
Defeated by a slave woman! I shall be
punished by my inferiors, it seems.

HECUBA

But justly so, since you committed evil.

POLYMESTOR

O my children!
And O light of my eyes!

HECUBA

It hurts, does it? And what of me? I mourn
my child too.

POLYMESTOR

Does it give you pleasure
to mock at me?

HECUBA

I rejoice in my revenge.

POLYMESTOR

Enjoy it now. You shall not enjoy it long.
Hear my prediction.
I foretell the seawaters . . .

HECUBA

Shall carry me on ship across to Greece?

POLYMESTOR

. . . shall drown you, after you fall from the masthead.

HECUBA

Who will force me to jump?

POLYMESTOR

You shall climb the mast
of your own free will . . .

HECUBA

Climb the mast? With wings?

POLYMESTOR

. . . changed to a dog, a bitch with blazing eyes.

HECUBA

How do you know of this transformation?

POLYMESTOR

Because our Thracian prophet, Dionysus,
told me so.

HECUBA

He neglected, I see, to foretell
your own woes.

POLYMESTOR

True: had he told my future then,
I never would have fallen into your trap.

HECUBA

Does the prophecy say I'll live or die?

POLYMESTOR

You'll die.
And when you die your tomb shall then be called . . .

HECUBA

In memory of my change, perhaps? Please tell me!

POLYMESTOR

. . . Cynossema, "the bitch's grave," a landmark
to sailors.

HECUBA

What do I care how I die?
I have my revenge.

POLYMESTOR

And your daughter Cassandra
must also die . . .

HECUBA

I spit your prophecies back.
Use them on yourself.

POLYMESTOR

. . . killed by this man's wife,
cut down by the bitter keeper of his house.

HECUBA

Clytemnestra? May she never be so crazed!

POLYMESTOR

Yes, she will lift the deadly axe on high
and kill this man, her husband, too.

AGAMEMNON

You're mad!
Are you asking for more trouble?

POLYMESTOR

Kill me,
but a bath of blood waits for you in Argos.

AGAMEMNON

Slaves, carry him off! Drag him away!

POLYMESTOR

Have I touched you now?

AGAMEMNON

Stop him. Gag his mouth.

POLYMESTOR

Gag me. I have spoken.

AGAMEMNON

Take him away
this instant.
Then throw him on some desert island
since his tongue cannot stop its impudence.

(Exit Polymestor to the side escorted by attendants.)

As for you, Hecuba, go now and bury
your two dead children.
You other Trojan women,
go to your masters' tents. For now I see
the sudden wind sits freshly in our sails.
May heaven grant that our ordeal is done

at last!
May all be well at home in Argos!

(Exit Agamemnon with remaining attendants to the side, Hecuba and her women with the corpse of Polydorus into the tent.)

CHORUS [*chanting*]
File to the tents,
file to the harbor.
There we embark
on life as slaves.
Necessity is harsh.
Fate has no reprieve.

THE SUPPLIANT WOMEN

Translated by FRANK WILLIAM JONES

THE SUPPLIANT WOMEN: INTRODUCTION

The Play: Date and Composition

It is not certain when Euripides' *Suppliant Women* was first produced, but scholars have used possible allusions in the play to contemporary political events and analysis of its metrical features to suggest a date between 424 and 420 BCE, perhaps 423 BCE. Presumably Euripides wrote it for the annual competition at the Great Dionysian Festival in Athens. What the other three plays were in Euripides' tetralogy of that year, and how they fared in the competition, are unknown.

The Myth

The Suppliant Women takes place in the aftermath of the attack of the Seven against Thebes. After Oedipus' removal from the throne, his sons Eteocles and Polynices could not share the rule of Thebes amicably, and Eteocles exiled Polynices to Argos. There Polynices raised an army that he and six other champions led to attack seven-gated Thebes. The Argive invaders were defeated and their champions slain—Eteocles and Polynices killed each other—and Creon, the new ruler of Thebes, adopted the extreme measure of refusing to grant them burial.

It is at this point that Euripides' play begins. Adrastus, the king of Argos, and the mothers and sons of the Seven come to Eleusis in Attica, where they ask the Athenians for help to bury their dead. They appeal first to Aethra, the mother of the Athenian king Theseus, and then to Theseus himself. Aethra overcomes Theseus' initial reluctance to help; Theseus then spurns the threats of a herald from Thebes; and in the subsequent battle Theseus and the Athenians are victorious over Creon and the Thebans. The bodies of the Seven are mourned by their relatives and eulogized by Adrastus; Evadne, the wife of Capaneus, one of the Seven, leaps to her death in his funeral pyre. The play concludes with the forecast of a second expedition against Thebes by the sons of the Seven and of an alliance between Argos and Athens.

Euripides' play combines two legendary themes, both of which were very popular and presumably well known to his audience. The first involves the vicissitudes of the Labdacids, the royal dynasty of Thebes: king Laius, his wife Jocasta, and their son Oedipus, and then their children Eteocles, Polynices, Antigone, and Ismene. The story had long been an important part of early Greek epic and oral legend. While the outline remained constant from version to version, the versions varied significantly in outcome, characterization, motivation, and moral evaluation. The myth was one of the most frequently dramatized in Attic tragedy. The attack of the Seven is presented in such plays as Aeschylus' *Seven against Thebes* and Euripides' *Phoenician Women* (written about 409 BCE) and is forecast in Sophocles' *Oedipus at Colonus*. The aftermath of their defeat, which forms the subject of Euripides' *Suppliant Women*, was also treated in Sophocles' *Antigone* among others.

The second theme of the play is Athens' acceptance of foreign suppliants and its military and religious protection of them against their enemies. This too is a kind of story popular among fifth-century Athenian audiences. Some years earlier, Euripides himself had treated an analogous legend in his *Children of Heracles* (written ca. 430 BCE), and Aeschylus in his lost *Eleusinians* had dramatized the very same events as the ones in Euripides' *Suppliant Women*. Broadly similar episodes also serve as the basis for Euripides' lost *Erechtheus* (written about the same time as his *Suppliant Women*) and Sophocles' *Oedipus at Colonus*. In addition, such patriotic stories of Athenian religiosity, generosity, and prowess were commonplaces among orators of this period, especially when commemorating Athenian soldiers who had fallen in combat. This particular story is not attested before the fifth century BCE and may well have been invented in Athens as a symbol of civic pride during Euripides' lifetime, though probably not by Euripides himself. Quite rightly, ancient scholars commented on *The Suppliant Women* that "the drama is an encomium of Athens."

Transmission and Reception

The Suppliant Women has never been one of Euripides' most popular plays. It survived antiquity only because it was one of the so-called "alphabetic plays" (see "Introduction to Euripides" in this volume, p. 3). Like the others in this group, it is transmitted only by a single manuscript in rather poor condition (and by its copies) and is not accompanied by the ancient commentaries (scholia) that explain various kinds of interpretative difficulties. Further evidence that it was not very popular in antiquity is that no papyri bearing any parts of its text have been discovered. The play has left little or no traces in ancient pictorial art; one Athenian cup, dated to about 430 BCE, has been found on which one of the mothers of the Seven is shown supplicating Theseus, but it is far from certain that the image should be linked to this play rather than to another version of the legend.

So too, the influence of the play on modern literature and art has been negligible.

THE SUPPLIANT WOMEN

Characters

AETHRA, mother of Theseus
THESEUS, king of Athens
ADRASTUS, king of Argos, and leader of the Seven against Thebes
A HERALD from Thebes, former servant of Capaneus
A MESSENGER from Thebes
EVADNE, widow of Capaneus, who fell in the war of the Seven against Thebes
IPHIS, her father
ATHENA
CHORUS: Mothers of the Seven against Thebes and their handmaids
SECOND CHORUS: A group of sons of the Seven against Thebes

Scene: The temple of Demeter and Persephone at Eleusis, near Athens.

(Enter Aethra. The Chorus of the Mothers of the Seven sit at her feet as suppliants, while Adrastus lies separately on the ground.)

AETHRA

Demeter, enshrined in this land Eleusis,
and you who tend the goddess' temple,
bless me and bless Theseus my son
and the city of Athens, and Pittheus' land,
where in prosperous halls my father reared me,

Aethra, and wed me to Pandion's son
Aegeus, as Loxias' oracle bade him.

So I pray as I look upon these women
burdened with years, who left their homes in Argos
to fall with suppliant branches at my feet
in dreadful loss: their seven noble sons
are dead at Cadmus' gates, and they are childless.
Adrastus, lord of Argos, led the men
to claim for his son-in-law, exiled Polynices,
a share of Oedipus' inheritance.
They perished in the struggle, and their mothers
desire to bury them; but those in power
spurn what the gods hold lawful and refuse
even to grant removal of the bodies.
The burden of these women's need for me
Adrastus also bears: look where he lies,
with tearful face mourning the grievous doom
that met the army he dispatched from home.
Through me he seeks a champion in my son
who shall prevail by words or force of arms
to take the dead and give them burial.
Only this he asks of my child and Athens.

I happen to be here for sacrifice
that the land be fruitful; I left my house
for this sanctuary, where first of all
the corn ear bristled above the ground.
And still I stay by the holy hearth
of the two goddesses, the Maiden and Demeter,
wearing a bondless bond of leaves,
in pity for these gray, childless mothers
and reverence for their sacred wreaths.
I have sent a herald to town, to summon
Theseus, that either he drive from the land
these people and the distress they bring,
or free them from their suppliant needs—

doing a pious action for the gods.
It is proper for women, if they are wise,
always to get things done by men.

CHORUS [*singing*]

STROPHE A

I appeal to you, old woman,
from aged mouth:
old, I fall at your knee.
Free my children°—
left by lawless men
to body-slackening death,
food for mountain beasts!

ANTISTROPHE A

See the piteous
tears at my eyelids
and wrinkled tearings of hands
at hoary flesh
because I could not lay out
my dead sons in my house
or see their tombs of earth!

STROPHE B

Gracious lady, you too once bore a son,
in blessing of the bed
for your husband: now to me
grant a part of your loving kindness,
in recompense for grievous pain
from the death of those I bore:
prevail, we beg, upon your son
that he go to Ismenus and bring to my hands
the bodies of the youthful dead that long for the tomb.

ANTISTROPHE B

Not for holy rites but in need I came
to fall and pray at the goddesses'
fire-receiving altars;

justice is ours, and you have power—
for you are happy in your child—
to take away my trouble.
My plight is pitiful: I beseech
your son to bring to these poor hands
the corpse, my son's sad limbs, for my embrace.

(Their handmaids begin to beat their breasts, scratch their cheeks, and wail in sign of mourning.)

STROPHE C

And now the strife of wailing, wailing!
Cry against cry, clashing of servants'[°] *hands!*
Let blows resound together!
Moan in the strain
of the dance that Hades loves!
Bloody the fingernail
along the white cheek, and stain the skin!
To mourn the dead
brings honor to those who live.

ANTISTROPHE C

Insatiable delight of wailing,
abounding in labor, carries me away,
as from a towering rock
cool water flows
unceasing ever: I wail,
for it is natural for women, when children die,
to undertake the labor of lament.
Ah! I only wish that in death
I might forget these griefs!

(Enter Theseus from the side.)

THESEUS

Whose are those wails I heard, and breast-beating,
and dirges for the dead? Here, from this temple,
the echoes came. Alarm takes hold of me:

my mother has been long away from home;
I come to find her; has she met with trouble?

Aha! What's there? I see strange things to speak of!
My aged mother sitting by the altar,
and foreign women with her, all awry
in shapes of woe: from age-dimmed eyes they shed
piteous tears to earth; their hair is shorn,
the robes they wear are not for festivals.
Mother, what does this mean? Yours to reveal,
mine to listen. I expect bad news.

AETHRA

These women, child, are mothers of the sons—
seven commanders—who died at Cadmus' gates;
and now with suppliant branches they watch and wait,
circled around me, as you see, my son.

THESEUS

And that man, groaning bitterly at the door?

AETHRA

They say he is Adrastus, lord of Argos.

THESEUS

And the boys beside him? Children of the women?

AETHRA

No, they are sons of the warriors who fell.

THESEUS

Why do they stretch out suppliant hands to us?

AETHRA

I know why; but it's for them to speak, my son.

THESEUS

You there, I call on you, you hidden beneath your cloak!
Leave off your wailing, bare your head and speak:
nothing advances without the tongue's help.

ADRASTUS

O Theseus, glorious victor king of Athens,
I come as suppliant to you and to your city.

THESEUS

What do you seek, and what is your need?

ADRASTUS

You know of my ruinous campaign?

THESEUS

Your passage through Greece was hardly silent.

ADRASTUS

In it I lost the finest men of Argos.

THESEUS

Such are the doings of wretched war.

ADRASTUS

I went to Thebes to request the dead be returned.

THESEUS

For burial, by the laws of war?

ADRASTUS

And now the ones who killed them will not let me.

THESEUS

What are their grounds? Your request is sacred.

ADRASTUS

They have no grounds. They are bad winners.

THESEUS

So you come to me for advice—or what?

ADRASTUS

I want you to bring back Argos' sons.

THESEUS

And where stands Argos? Are her boasts in vain?

ADRASTUS

Defeated, finished. So we come to you.

THESEUS
By your design alone, or the whole city's?

ADRASTUS
All Danaus' descendants beg you to bury our dead.

THESEUS
Why did you march those seven bands against Thebes?

ADRASTUS
To please the men who married my two daughters.

THESEUS
To which of the Argives did you give your children?

ADRASTUS
The bond I formed was not among my kin.

THESEUS
To strangers, then, you wedded Argive girls?

ADRASTUS
Yes: to Tydeus, and to Theban Polynices.

THESEUS
How did you come to want them for your kin?

ADRASTUS
Puzzling riddles of Phoebus lured me on.

THESEUS
What words of Apollo meant marriage for the maidens?

ADRASTUS
That I give my daughters to a boar and a lion.

THESEUS
And how did you unravel the god's pronouncement?

ADRASTUS
A pair of exiles came to my door at night . . .

THESEUS
What pair? You speak of two at once: explain.

ADRASTUS

. . . Tydeus and Polynices, and fought each other.

THESEUS

They were the beasts? You gave your girls to them?

ADRASTUS

Yes, they looked like two wild creatures fighting.

THESEUS

Why had they left the borders of their countries?

ADRASTUS

Tydeus in guilt of shedding kindred blood.

THESEUS

And what brought Oedipus' son away from Thebes?

ADRASTUS

A father's curse: that he would kill his brother.

THESEUS

Then voluntary flight was wise of him.

ADRASTUS

True; but those remaining wronged the absent.

THESEUS

You mean his brother robbed him of his goods?

ADRASTUS

To punish that wrong I went to Thebes, and lost.

THESEUS

You asked the seers, and watched their sacrificial flames?

ADRASTUS

Ah! You pursue me where my case is weakest.

THESEUS

The gods, it seems, did not approve your mission.

ADRASTUS

I also flouted Amphiaraus' will.

THESEUS

So lightly you ignored the gods' own signs?

ADRASTUS

Unruliness of youthful men confused me.

THESEUS

You followed strength of heart, not strength of mind.

ADRASTUS

This is a course that ruins many generals.°
But lord of Athens! Crown of power in Hellas!
I am ashamed—a gray-haired man who once
was king, and fortunate—that now I fall
to earth and clasp your knee; and yet I must
submit to my disaster. Save my dead!
Have pity on my woes, and on these mothers
of fallen sons! Struck childless in old age
with feeble limbs they come to a strange land—
not to attend Demeter's mysteries,
but seeking burial of the dead whose hands,
in pious duty, should have buried them.
The sight of poverty is wise for wealth;
the poor should gaze with envy on the rich,
to learn the love of goods; untroubled men
are well advised to look at wretchedness.°
The poet bringing songs into the world
should work in joy. If this is not his mood,
he cannot—being inwardly distressed—
give pleasure outwardly. That stands to reason.
You may well ask: "Why pass by Pelops' land,
and seek to lay this task of yours on Athens?"
In fairness, I would make this answer. Sparta
is savage; its ways are devious; and the others
are small and weak. Yours is the only city
with strength enough to undertake the task:
Athens sees what misery is, and as its leader

has you, a good and youthful shepherd. Ruin
has come to many states that lack such leadership.

CHORUS LEADER

Theseus! I join my prayer to his:
pity my wretchedness.

THESEUS

I have heard such arguments before, from others,
and fought them hard. It has been said that life
holds more of worse conditions than of better;
but I oppose that doctrine. I believe
the good outweighs the bad in human life.
If it did not, the light would not be ours.
I praise the god who set our life in order,
lifting it out of savagery and confusion.
First he put wits in us, and then gave language,
envoy of words, to understand the voice;
and fruits of earth to eat, and for this food
watery drops from heaven, to quench our thirst
and nourish the yield of the land; providing also
defense against winter, against the sun god's fire,
and commerce over sea, that by exchange
a country may obtain the goods it lacks.
Things without mark, not clearly understood,
are brought to light by seers who study fire,
the folds of entrails, and the flight of birds.
Now, if all this is not enough for us—
so well equipped for living, by the god's gift—
are we not spoiled and greedy? And yet arrogance
wants more than godly power; our minds grow proud,
until we think we are wiser than the gods.
  That is the brand of unwisdom you have shown.
First, bowing to Phoebus' words, like one who thinks
the gods gave them,° you gave your girls to strangers:
a mating of fair with foul, to hurt your house!
Wrongdoers' bodies should not be joined to the just;

a wise man will ally his family
with well-regarded people. For when fortunes are shared
in common, a man who has done no wrong
and is not sick may be destroyed by the gods
together with his truly diseased neighbor.
Then, when you took
all Argos with you on that expedition,
the seers spoke omens but you slighted them,
flouted the gods, and laid your city low.
You were led astray by glory-loving youngsters,
promoters of unjust wars, who ruin the townsmen.
One of them wants to be a general;
another to seize power and riot in it;
a third is set on gain. They never think
what harm this brings for the majority.
The classes of citizens are three. The rich
are useless, always lusting after more.
Those who have not, and live in want, are a menace,
ridden with envy and fooled by demagogues;
their malice stings the owners. Of the three,
the middle part saves cities: it guards the order
a community establishes.
And so
I am to be your ally? What fine words
will make my citizens favor that? Farewell!
You planned your actions poorly. Take what comes:
wrestle with fate alone, and let us be.°

CHORUS LEADER

He blundered. That is natural in the young,
and should be pardoned in him. We have come
to you, my lord, as healer of these ills.°

ADRASTUS

In choosing you, my lord, I did not think
that you would sit in judgment on my woes,
or estimate and punish any act

of wickedness I may have carried out;
I only wanted help. If you refuse,
I have no choice; I must obey.
Now, aged ladies, please go forth. Lay down
your branches green with foliage on this spot,
calling to witness gods and earth and sun
and Queen Demeter, bearer of the torch,
that prayers to the gods have availed us nothing.

CHORUS LEADER

O King, you are of Pelops' line, and we are from his country:°
the same ancestral blood is ours. How can it be
that you forsake this cause, and drive out of your land
old women who have gained nothing that is owed them?
We pray you not to do this. Beasts have rocks for refuge;
slaves, the altars of the gods; city huddles with city
when storms come. Nothing mortal prospers to the end.

CHORUS [*singing*]

Woman of sorrows! Leave Persephone's sacred ground;°
go up to him and throw your arms about his knees;
beg him to bring your sons' dead bodies—Oh, the grief!
The young men whom I lost beneath Cadmean walls.
Alas! these poor old hands: take them, guide them, support them.°
Friend! Honor and glory of Hellas! I touch your beard;
here at your knees I fall and seek your hand in my woe.
If you would shelter a wanderer,° pity me—
suppliant for my children, piteously lamenting.
Child! I appeal to you: you are young, do not leave my sons
unburied in Cadmus' land, to gladden the wild beasts!
I fall and clasp your knees: see the tears at my eyelids!
I beg you, bring to fulfillment the burial of my children!

THESEUS

Mother: you hold your finespun cloak to your eyes.
Why do you weep? Is it because you hear
the lamentations uttered by these women?

Somehow, they pierce me too. Raise your white head:
no more tears, at Demeter's sacred hearth!

AETHRA

Ah!

THESEUS

Their troubles should not make you moan.

AETHRA

Poor women!

THESEUS

You do not belong to them.

AETHRA

Child! May I speak, for the city's good and yours?

THESEUS

Many wise things are said even by women.

AETHRA

I shrink from showing what I have in mind.

THESEUS

It is shameful to hold back words that might help your kin.

AETHRA

I would not now be still, and afterward
blame myself for a silence wrongly kept;
or fear that women's well-meant words are wasted,
and in that dread let my goodwill be lost.
My child, I bid you: first, look to the gods;
for if you slight them you will fall. Intentions
good in themselves are wrecked by that one fault.°
If you weren't asked to launch an enterprise
in order to help those wronged, then certainly
I would be silent. But you must be told
how greatly it would honor you (so much
that I am not afraid to urge it, child!)
if cruel men, who would deny the dead

the rights of burial and their funerals,
were forced to grant this, by your hand, and stopped
from violating what all Greece holds lawful.
The power that keeps cities of men together
is noble preservation of the laws.
It will be said that, lacking manly strength,
you stood aside in fear and lost a chance
to win a crown of glory for the city.
They will say you hunted boars, a mean pursuit,
and proved a coward at the call of action,
the time for spear and helmet. Child of mine,
this must not be! Remember your descent!
Do you see your country's Gorgon stare when taunted
with lack of resolution? Athens thrives
on strenuous action; but those cautious states
that do their work in darkness wear a somber look
to match their caution. Child, won't you go to help
the dead, and these poor women in their need?
It is a just campaign; and I have no fear:
the sons of Cadmus now have been successful,
but soon the dice will fall another way.
I hold this certain. God reverses all.

CHORUS LEADER

O best-loved lady! Nobly have you spoken,
for him and me, giving a double joy.

THESEUS

Mother, what I have said now to this man
I still consider right. I spoke my mind
on the designs that led him to his ruin.
But I also see the truth of what you tell me:
that it is not in keeping with my ways
to run from risk. By many noble deeds
I have made myself a byword to the Greeks:
they count on me to punish wickedness.
I am unable to refuse a task.

What then will hostile persons say of me
if you, my mother, you who fear for me,
are the first to urge me to undertake this labor?
Forward, then; I shall go and free the dead.
Persuasion first: if that does not succeed,
then force of arms will gain my end. The gods
will not be jealous. I desire the city
with all its voices to approve this plan.
It will approve because I want it to:
but if I state my reasons, I shall have
more favor from the people, whom I made
sole rulers when I set their city free
and gave them equal votes. So I shall take
Adrastus to support my argument
and go to all the citizens assembled,
convince them that this must be done, pick out
a group of young Athenians, and return.
Then, resting on my weapons, I shall send
to ask the bodies of the dead from Creon.
Matrons: take off these garlands from my mother.
I must conduct her to the house of Aegeus,
clasping her loving hand. I think it wrong
that a child should not return his parents' care.
Noblest of gifts! By granting it, he earns
from his own children what he gives his elders.

(Exit Theseus, Adrastus, and Aethra to the side.)

CHORUS [*singing*]

STROPHE A

Argos, my fatherland, pasture of horses:
you heard him speak, you heard from the king
words that respect the gods,
words that mean greatness for Greece and Argos.

ANTISTROPHE A

May he go to the end of my woes, and beyond;
may he rescue the mother's bloodstained precious

darling, and thus make friendship
firm with the land of Inachus.

STROPHE B

A work of piety brings honor and glory to cities
and earns thanks that last forever.
What dare I hope from the city? Will it truly give
a pledge of friendship for me, and graves for my sons?

ANTISTROPHE B

City of Pallas! A mother begs you to protect her and prevent
the desecration of human law.
You revere right, despise crime, and are ready
always to help the unfortunate.

(Enter from the side Theseus, Adrastus, and an Athenian herald.)

THESEUS *(To the herald.)*

The skill you have as bearer of proclamations
has given constant service to me and the city.
Now you must cross the streams Asopus and Ismenus
and tell the haughty ruler of the Cadmeans this:
"Theseus asks you, by your grace, to bury the dead. His country
neighbors yours, and he believes the request is worth the granting.
Do this and you will have all of Erechtheus' people for friends."
If they consent, commend them and hasten back.
If they refuse, deliver a second message:
"Welcome my band of revelers, men who carry shields!"
A ready task force waits, under review,
here and now at the sacred Fount of the Dance.
The city, when it saw I willed this effort,
was ready to accept it, even glad.

(Enter from the other side a Theban Herald.)

But who comes here, to interrupt my words?
I cannot tell for sure; he seems to be

a Theban herald. Stay a while. His coming
might fit my plans, and you would be released.

HERALD

What man is master in this land? To whom
must I give the word I bring from Creon, ruler
in Cadmus' country since Eteocles
fell at his brother Polynices' hand
beside the seven-mouthed gates?

THESEUS

One moment, stranger.
Your start was wrong, seeking a master here.
This city is free, and ruled by no one man.
The people reign, in annual alternations.
And they do not yield the power to the rich;
the poor man has an equal share in it.

HERALD

That one point gives the better of the game
to me. The town I come from is controlled
by one man, not a mob. And there is no one
to puff it up with words, for private gain,
swaying it this way, that way. Such a man
first flatters it with wealth of favors; then
he does it harm, but covers up his blunders
by blaming other men, and goes scot-free.
The people are no right judge of arguments;
so how can they give right guidance to a city?
For time, not speed, gives better understanding.
A poor man, working hard, could not attend
to public matters, even if ignorance
were not his birthright. When a wretch, a nothing,
obtains respect and power from the people
by talk, his betters sicken at the sight.

THESEUS

What bombast from a herald! Waster of words,

if it is argument you want—and you yourself
have set the contest going—listen.
Nothing
is worse for a city than an absolute ruler.
For first, if so, there are no common laws:
one man has power and makes the law his own;
there's no equality. With written laws,
people of small resources and the rich
both have the same recourse to justice. So°
a man of means, if badly spoken of,
will have no better standing than the weak;
and if the little man is right, he wins
against the great. This is the call of freedom:
"What man has good advice to give the city,
and wishes to make it known?" He who responds
gains glory; the reluctant hold their peace.
For the city, what can be more fair than that?
Again, when the people are master in the land,
they welcome youthful townsmen as their subjects;
but when one man is king, he finds this hateful,
and if he thinks that any of the nobles
are smart, he fears for his despotic power
and kills them. How can a city become strong
if someone takes away, cuts off bold youths
like ears of corn in a spring field? What use
to build a fortune, if your work promotes
the despot's welfare, not your family's?
Why bring up girls well and modestly, fit
for marriage, if tyrants may take them for their pleasure—
a grief to parents? I would rather die
than see my children forced to such a union.
These are the responses I shoot at what you say.
What have you come to ask of this, our country?
You talk too much; you would regret your visit
had not a city sent you. Messengers
should state their mission promptly, then depart.

I hope that henceforth, to my city, Creon
sends a less wordy messenger than you.

CHORUS LEADER

When fortune aids the wicked, how they revel!
They act as if their luck would last forever.

HERALD

Now I shall speak. On what has been debated,
you may hold your views, I the opposite.
I and the whole Cadmean people say
Adrastus must not pass into this land.
If he has entered it, you must strip off
his sacred ritual wreaths and drive him out
before the sun god's flame has set. His dead
must not be removed by force; the Argives' city
is no concern of yours. Do what I say
and you will steer your city's course in calm.
If you refuse, there will be much rough water
for us, for you, and for our allies: war.
Think now: do not let anger at my words
goad you to puffed-up answers. You are free;
that does not make you powerful. Hope has driven
many cities against each other; it stirs
an overreaching heart; it is not to be trusted.
When the people vote on war, nobody reckons
on his own death; it is too soon; he thinks
some other man will meet that wretched fate.
But if death were before his eyes when he cast his vote,
Hellas would never be ruined by battle-madness.
And yet we men all know which of two speeches
is better, and can weigh the good and bad
they bring: how much better is peace than war!
First and foremost, the Muses love her best;
and the goddess of vengeance hates her. Peace delights
in healthy children, and she glories in wealth.
But evilly we throw all this away

to start our wars and make the losers slaves—
man binding man and city shackling city.
And you would help our enemies in death,
taking away for burial men who fell
by their own insolence? Don't you think it right
that thunderbolts made smoke of Capaneus,
the one who thrust the ladders at the gates
and swore to sack the city whether god
willed it or not? The bird interpreter,
was he not swallowed by a gulf that opened
around his four-horse chariot? There they lie,
the other squadron leaders, by the gates;
rocks have crushed the framework of their bones.
So either boast a greater mind than Zeus,
or grant that the gods punish the bad justly.
Wise men should cherish their children first, then parents,
then their country—and that they ought to strengthen,
not devastate. A bold leader or sailor
brings peril; the man who knows when not to act
is wise. To my mind, bravery is forethought.

CHORUS LEADER

Zeus the punisher was enough. No need
for you to gloat like this over their downfall.

ADRASTUS

You miserable wretch—

THESEUS

Silence, Adrastus!
Restrain yourself. Do not give precedence
to your words over mine. This message comes
to me, not you; and I must answer it.

(To the Herald.)

First I shall answer what you stated first.
I have not heard that Creon is my master,

or that he has more power than I. How then
can he compel Athens to do his bidding?
If we serve him, the world runs backward! I
did not begin this war: I was not with them
when they invaded Thebes; I only think it just
to bury their dead. I mean no harm to the city,
no man-destroying struggles: I uphold
the law of all the Greeks. Is that unfair?
Yes, certainly the Argives caused you harm,
but they are dead. You fought them off with honor,
to their disgrace; and now the case is closed.
Come! Let the dead be covered by the ground,
and let each part regain the element
from which it came to light: the spirit, air;
the body, earth. The flesh is only ours
to dwell in while life lasts; and afterward
the giver of its strength must take it back.
Do you think to hurt Argos by leaving her dead unburied?
You miss your target. All Hellas is concerned
when anyone tries to strip the dead of their due
and keep them from the tomb. If that were custom,
brave men would turn cowards. And yet you come
to threaten me with frightful words. Do you dread
the corpses? If they are hidden in earth, what then?
Will they overthrow your country from the grave,
or beget children in the womb of earth
who will avenge them some day? Fears like these
are base and vain, a waste of breath to speak.
Fools! Be instructed in the ills of man.
Struggles make up our life. Good fortune came
formerly to some, to some hereafter; others
enjoy it now. Its god luxuriates.
Not only is he honored by the hapless
in hope of better days, but lucky ones
exalt him too, fearing that they'll lose
the favorable breeze.

Aware of this, you should not take it hard
when moderately wronged, or do a wrong
so great that it will hurt your city. Therefore
you ought to grant the bodies of the fallen
to us, who wish to do them reverence.
If you choose otherwise, my course is clear:
I shall compel their burial. Never shall
the Greeks have this news to hear: that ancient law,
established by the gods, appealed to me
and Pandion's city, only to be annulled.

CHORUS LEADER

Courage! Keep alive the light of justice,
and much that men say in blame will pass you by.

HERALD

May I make a speech that is short and plain?

THESEUS

Say what you like: you're not the silent type.

HERALD

You will never take Argos' sons from my country.

THESEUS

Now hear me, if you will, in turn.

HERALD

I listen; I must grant your due.

THESEUS

I shall bury the dead away from Thebes.

HERALD

First you must risk a clash of shields.

THESEUS

I have come through many other trials.

HERALD

Did your father make you a match for all comers?

THESEUS
For offenders, yes; I do not crush virtue.

HERALD
You and your city are busybodies.

THESEUS
By laboring hard she earns prosperity.

HERALD
Go, and be killed by a Sown Man's spear!

THESEUS
What warlike fury can come from a dragon?

HERALD
Feel it and know it. You are still young.

THESEUS
You cannot rouse my mind to wrath
by boasting. Take the foolish words
you brought, and leave the country. Talk
will gain us nothing.

(Exit the Theban Herald to the side.)

Forward, every man
who fights on foot, on horse, or from a chariot!
Let cheek-pieces rattle, flecking the horses' mouths
with foam as they gallop toward the Theban land!
I march on Cadmus' seven gates; I bear
sharp iron in my hand and act as herald
on my behalf. Adrastus, I command you,
stay here; do not attach your fate to me.
I shall lead the army, guided by my god,
as a new commander with a new armed force.
Only one thing I need: to have with me
the gods who honor justice. That support
gives victory. Human excellence means nothing
unless it works with the consent of god.

(*Exit Theseus to the side.*)

CHORUS [*singing one to another*]°

STROPHE A

Pitiful mothers of lost commanders!
Yellow fear sits on my heart.°

—*What new word is this you bring?*

—*How will the mission of Pallas stand the test?*

—*By fighting, did you say, or exchange of words?*

—*I pray that goodwill come of it!*
But what if it ends in slaughters by Ares,
battles, din of beaten breasts throughout the city?
Then what could I find to say,
I, who caused it all?

ANTISTROPHE A

—*The man who glories in his luck*
may be overthrown by destiny;
in that hope I rest secure.

—*Then you believe in gods who stand for justice.*

—*Of course; what other beings make such things happen?*

—*I see great difference between the gods and mortals.*

—*That is because you are crushed by fear*
from the past. But justice has called for justice, blood for blood;
the gods, who hold in their hands the end of all,
give men rest from pain.

—*How might we leave this sacred fount of the goddess*
and reach Thebes' plains with the beautiful towers?

STROPHE B

—*If one of the gods would give you wings . . .*
—*. . . on the way to the two-rivered city.*

—You would know, then you would know how our friends are faring.
—What destiny, what turn of fate, I wonder,
is waiting for this country's mighty lord?

ANTISTROPHE B

—Again we call on gods we invoked already:
here is the foremost hope of the frightened.
—O Zeus, who fathered a child for the heifer
daughter of Inachus, mother of old,
favor this my city and help its cause.
Your glory, the city's mainstay, has been outraged;
bring him back, I pray, to be readied for the pyre.

(Enter a Messenger from Thebes, from the side.)

MESSENGER

Women, I bring much news that you will welcome.
I have come through to safety after capture
in the battle which the seven companies
of fallen masters fought by Dirce's stream.
I am here to tell of Theseus' victory.
To spare you long inquiry: I was a servant
of Capaneus, whom Zeus's flaming bolt
riddled to ashes.

CHORUS LEADER

Oh, with joy we greet
your news of coming home, and hear the word
you bring of Theseus! If Athens' army too
is safe, then all you have to tell is welcome.

MESSENGER

Safe; and it did what should have been achieved
by Adrastus with the Argives when he marched
from Inachus against the Cadmean city.

CHORUS LEADER

How did the son of Aegeus and his comrades

gain victory? Tell us now. You saw it happen;
you can give joy to those who were not there.

MESSENGER

A brilliant shaft of sunlight, straight and clear,
lit up the field as I stood at Electra gate,
where a tower gave a sweeping view. I saw
three forces marshaled. Infantry with armor
extended toward high ground: the Ismenian hill,
I heard it called. The famous son of Aegeus,
with men from old Cecropia held the right;
the left wing, spear-armed Coast men, took positions
beside the Spring of Ares. Cavalry massed
at each wing's end, in equal groups; and chariots
stood at the foot of Amphion's sacred mound.
Cadmus' men, posted before the walls, had put
the corpses, cause of conflict, at their rear.
Horsemen faced horsemen; chariots stood ready,
equipped to battle four-horse chariots.
Then Theseus' herald spoke these words to all:
"Silence, my men; silence, Cadmean troops.
Hear me: we come to take the dead. We wish
to bury them, and so uphold the law
of all the Greeks. It is not our desire
to shed more blood." Creon gave no command
to answer this, but sat in silence, ready.
Then the charioteers began the combat.
Driving their chariots toward and past each other,
they set their fighters down, in line of battle.
While these crossed swords, the drivers turned their horses
back to support their men. When Phorbas, captain
of Athens' horsemen, and the overseers
of Theban cavalry saw the chariots clustered,
they threw their forces into the tide of war,
now one side gaining advantage, now the other.

As witness, not from hearsay—I was close
to the battleground of chariots and riders—
I know the many sufferings there, but not
where to begin. With the dust that rose toward heaven?
How thick it was! Or men tossed up and down,
caught in the horses' reins? Or streams of blood
from men who fell, or were flung headfirst to earth
when cars were shattered, leaving their life beside
wreckage of chariots? When Creon saw
our mounted forces winning, he took his shield
and advanced to keep his allies from despair.
Then all the middle of the field was spattered
as men slew and were slain; and the word passed,
shouted aloud among them: "Strike! Thrust back
the spear at Erechtheus' sons!" But Theseus' fortunes
were not to fall by delaying. Snatching up
his shining arms, he charged at once. Fiercely
the host that grew to men from dragon's teeth
opposed us, pushing our left wing back; but theirs
lost to our right and fled. The scales of war
stood even. Then our general earned praise;
not seeking only to follow up advantage,
he hurried to his forces' breaking point,
shouting so loud that he made the earth resound:
"Hold, lads, against these dragon men's stiff spears,
or else farewell to Athens!" That stirred courage
throughout the Cranaid army. Then he seized
his Epidaurian weapon, a ghastly club,
and swung it right and left, dealing his blows
on heads and necks together; the massive cudgel
mowed off and snapped their helmets; turning to flee,
they could hardly move their feet. I rejoiced and danced
and clapped my hands. The Thebans made for the gates.
Then there were cries and groans throughout the city
from young and old; frightened, they thronged the temples.

Now Theseus might have gone inside the walls;
but he held back, declaring that his purpose
was not to sack the town but claim the dead.
That is the kind of general to elect:
one who puts forth his strength in time of danger,
and hates an insolent people that keeps climbing
to the ladder's top even when times are good
and wrecks the happiness it might enjoy.

CHORUS LEADER

Now, having seen this day, surpassing hope,
I believe in gods. The lesser share of evil
seems to be mine now; Thebes has paid the price.

ADRASTUS

Zeus! Who dares call us hapless mortals wise?
You dangle us; whatever you want, we do.
Argos, we thought, was irresistible:
we were so many, young, and strong of arm!
Eteocles would have come to terms; his offer
was fair; but we refused, and lost.
The winners then, the malignant folk of Cadmus,
ran riot like a pauper newly rich;
but now their rioting brings them down, in turn.
O you who try to shoot beyond the mark,
you mindless mortals! Richly you deserve
your many woes; you listen not to friends,
but to your interests. Cities! You might use
reason to end your troubles; but instead
with blood, not words, you ruin your affairs.—Enough!

(To the Messenger.)

I would like to know how you reached safety;
then I will ask my other questions.

MESSENGER

When the city shook in turmoil of war,
I went through the gates where the troops came in.

ADRASTUS

Do you bring the dead for whom they fought?

MESSENGER

Yes, the captains of the seven armies.

ADRASTUS

But the mass of the fallen—where are they?

MESSENGER

Buried near Cithaeron's folds.

ADRASTUS

This side, or that? By whom were they buried?

MESSENGER

At Eleutherae's shady ridge. By Theseus.

ADRASTUS

Those he did not bury—where have you left them?

MESSENGER

Close by. Speed makes all roads short.

ADRASTUS

Did it pain the servants to bring them out of the carnage?

MESSENGER

No one who was a slave had charge of that.

ADRASTUS

Did Theseus welcome the task?°

MESSENGER

You would have said so
if you had seen his loving salute to the dead.

ADRASTUS

And did he wash the victims' wounds himself?

MESSENGER

He even spread the biers and covered the bodies.

ADRASTUS

That was a dreadful burden, bringing shame.

MESSENGER

How can humanity's common ills be shameful?

ADRASTUS

Oh, how much rather had I died with them!

MESSENGER

Your laments are vain, and make these women weep.

ADRASTUS

Yes. It was they who taught me. Now I cease.
I'll go and raise my hand when I meet the dead,
and speak, in long and tearful chants of Hades,
to friends by whom I am left to mourn alone.
If you lose money you can get it back, but no one
recovers this expense: a human life.

(Exit Adrastus and Messenger to the side.)

CHORUS [*singing*]

STROPHE A

Part well, part ill—this turn of fate.
For city and generals who went to war,
glory and honor redoubled;
for me, to look upon my children's bodies—
a bitter, lovely sight, if ever I see it,
and the day despaired of,
greatest pain of all.

ANTISTROPHE A

Would that old Time, father of days,
had left me unwed all my life.
What need had I of children?
Once, I thought, I could not bear the sorrow
of being barred from marriage. Now
the loss of dearest children
is an evil plain to see.

(Enter Theseus and Adrastus from the side with attendants, bearing the five corpses of the fallen chiefs.)

[*chanting*]
The woeful sight has come: my fallen children's bodies!
Oh, to join them in death and go down to Hades together!

ADRASTUS [*singing throughout this lyric interchange, with the Chorus singing in reply*]

STROPHE B

Mothers! Wail for the dead who are underground!
Wail in answer when you hear my moans!

CHORUS
Children! I bid you now in death
a bitter farewell from loving mothers.

ADRASTUS
O grief, O grief!

CHORUS
For my own woes I cry.°

ADRASTUS
We have borne . . .

CHORUS
. . . the most tormenting evils.

ADRASTUS
O Argive city! Do your folk not see my downfall?

CHORUS
They see me too in my wretched state, barren of children.

ADRASTUS

ANTISTROPHE B

Bring on the bloodstained bodies of the doomed—
champions in war, laid low by lesser men.

CHORUS

Give me my children to take in my arms;
my hands are ready for that embrace.

ADRASTUS

You have and hold . . .

CHORUS

. . . burden enough of woes.

ADRASTUS

Alas!

CHORUS

No word for the mothers?

ADRASTUS

Hear me.

CHORUS

You groan with your pain and mine.

ADRASTUS

I wish the Theban columns had struck me down in the dust.

CHORUS

Would that my body had never been yoked to a husband's bed.

ADRASTUS

EPODE

O wretched mothers of children!
Behold, a sea of troubles.

CHORUS

Our nails cut furrows down our cheeks;
we have poured dust over our heads.

ADRASTUS

Oh, oh, ah me!
Swallow me, earth!
Whirlwind, tear me apart!
Blaze of Zeus's fire, swoop down upon me!

CHORUS

Bitter the wedding you saw,
bitter the word of Phoebus;
a Fury, bringer of grief,
has abandoned Oedipus' house and come to yours.

→ demon things had oedipus's family now Adrastus

THESEUS

Before your long lament in front of the army°
I would have asked you this, but I refrained
from speaking then, and so I let it pass.
But now, Adrastus, I ask: these are men whose spirit
has brought them fame. What is their lineage?
Speak, from your greater knowledge, to the young
among our citizens; you have understanding.°
One thing I ask not, or you'd laugh at me;
who it was that each warrior stood and fought against,
or from which foe he took a spear wound. Vain
to tell or hear such tales—as if a man
in the thick of combat, with a storm of spears
before his eyes, ever brought back sure news
on who was hero. I can neither ask
such questions nor believe those who make bold
to answer them. When you stand against the foe,
it is hard enough to see what must be seen.

ADRASTUS

Hear, then. By granting me the privilege
of praising friends, you meet my own desire
to speak of them with justice and with truth.
I saw the deeds—bolder than words can tell—°
by which they hoped to take the city.
Look:
this dead one here is Capaneus. Through him
a fierce lightning bolt went. A man of means, he never
flaunted his wealth but kept an attitude
no prouder than a poor man's. He avoided
people who live beyond their needs and load

their tables to excess. He used to say
that good does not consist in belly-food,
and satisfaction comes from moderation.
He was true in friendship to present and absent friends;
not many men are so. His character
was never false; his ways were courteous;
his doings, in house or city, were always modest.
Second I name Eteoclus. He practiced
another kind of virtue. Though he lacked means,
this youth held many offices in Argos.
Often his friends would offer to give him gold,
but he never took it into his house. He wanted
no slavish way of life, haltered by money.
He kept his hate for wrongdoers, not the city;
a town is not to blame if a bad pilot
makes men speak ill of it.
Hippomedon,
third of the heroes, showed his nature thus:
while yet a boy he had the strength of will
not to take up the pleasures of the Muses
that soften life; he went to live in the country,
giving himself hard tasks to do, rejoicing
in manly deeds. He hunted, delighted in horses,
and stretched the bow with his hands, to make his body
useful to the city.
There lies the son
of huntress Atalanta, Parthenopaeus,
supreme in beauty. He was Arcadian,
but came to Inachus' banks and was reared in Argos.
After his upbringing there, he showed himself,
as resident foreigners should, not troublesome
or spiteful to the city, or disputatious,
which is what makes one hardest to tolerate
as citizen and guest. He joined the army
like a born Argive, fought the country's wars,

was glad when the city prospered, took it hard
if bad times came. Although he had many lovers,
and women flocked to him,° still he was careful
to do them all no wrong.
                                                  In praise of Tydeus
I shall say much in little.° He was ambitious,
greatly gifted, and wise in deeds, not words.
   From what I have told you, Theseus, you should not wonder
that these men dared to die before the towers.
To be well brought up develops self-respect:
anyone who has practiced what is good
is ashamed to turn out badly. Manliness
is teachable. Even a child is taught
to say and hear what he does not yet understand;
things understood are kept in mind till age.
So, in like manner, train your children well.

CHORUS [*singing*]
O my child, to an evil fate I bred you,
carried you in my womb
and felt the pangs of birth!
Now, alas! Hades holds my burden,
and I have none to cherish me in age,
though I bore a child, to my sorrow.

THESEUS
And what of Oecles' noble son? His praises
are uttered by the gods, who bore him off
alive, with his chariot, into the depths of earth.
I too, in all sincerity, might honor
Oedipus' son: I speak of Polynices.
Before he left Cadmus' town, he stayed with me
till he chose Argos for his place of exile.
Now, do you know what I wish to do with the fallen?

ADRASTUS
This only I know—to obey your orders.

THESEUS

Capaneus, struck by Zeus's fire—

ADRASTUS

You will bury apart, as a sacred corpse?

THESEUS

Yes. But one pyre for all the others.

ADRASTUS

Where will you set his single memorial?

THESEUS

Beside this shrine I will build the tomb.

ADRASTUS

The slaves will look to that labor now.

THESEUS

And I to the rest. Bearers, move on.

ADRASTUS

Sorrowful mothers! Draw near your children!

THESEUS

Adrastus! That was not well said.

ADRASTUS

Why? Must the parents not touch their children?

THESEUS

To see their state would be mortal pain.

ADRASTUS

Yes; corpse wounds and blood are a bitter sight.

THESEUS

Then why would you increase the women's woe?

ADRASTUS

I yield.

(To the women.)

You must be brave, and stay where you are.
Theseus is right. When we have put them to the fire,
you will take home their bones. O wretched mortals,
why do you slaughter each other with your spears?
Leave off those struggles; let your towns take shelter
in gentleness. Life is a short affair;
we should try to make it smooth, and free from strife.

(Exit to the side Theseus, Adrastus, the sons of the Seven, and the funeral procession.)

CHORUS [*singing*]

STROPHE

Blest no more with children, blest no more with sons,
I have no share in happiness
among the boy-bearing women of Argos.
And Artemis, who watches over birth,
would have no word for childless women.
My life is a time of woe;
I am like a wandering cloud
sent hurtling by fierce winds.

ANTISTROPHE

Seven mothers, we gave birth to seven sons
who gained the heights of fame in Argos;
but that has brought us suffering.
And now, without a son, without a child,
most miserably I grow old,
neither a living creature
nor one of the dead, my fate
something apart from both.

EPODE

Tears are left to me; sad
memorials of my son are in my house:
locks shorn from my hair, and no wreaths for me, in mourning,
libations for the vanished dead, and songs

unwelcome to golden-haired Apollo.
At every dawn I shall wake to weep
and drench the folds of my dress at the breast with tears.

(*Enter Evadne above the temple.*)

[*chanting*]
Already I can see the vaults
of the sacred tomb of Capaneus,
and Theseus' memorials to the dead, outside the temple.
And close at hand I see Evadne,
famous wife of him who died by lightning,
daughter of Iphis the king.
Why has she climbed that path
to stand on a lofty rock
that towers above this shrine?

EVADNE [*singing*]

STROPHE

Over what blaze, what gleam did sun and moon°
drive their chariots through the air
where the light-bringers ride,
on that dark day when Argos' city
built towers of song and greetings
for my wedding and the bridegroom,
bronze-armored Capaneus? Ah!
To you I come, wildly running from home!
I shall enter the glow of the pyre and share your grave,
making Hades my release
from the weary weight of life
and the pain of being.
This is the sweetest death: to die with loved ones dying,
if a god should so decree.

CHORUS LEADER
You see this pyre; you stand above and near it;
it is the treasure-house of Zeus. There lies
your husband, victim of the lightning flash.

EVADNE [*singing*]

ANTISTROPHE

From here I see where I shall end.°
Fortune guides the leap of my feet to glory.
From this rock I will dive
into the flames. My body will mingle
in fiery glow with my husband,
his loved flesh close to mine.
So shall I come to Persephone's halls,
resolved never to cheat your death by living
upon this earth. Daylight, wedlock, farewell!
May better fortune attend Argive marriages
shown to be true by my children!
Devoted husband,
may you dwell happy, drawn to your noble wife
by steady winds of love!

(*Enter Iphis from the side.*)

CHORUS LEADER

Your father, aged Iphis, comes upon
strange words, unheard-of, that will hurt to hear.

IPHIS

O women of sorrows! To my sorrowful age
my family has brought a double grief.
I have come to take my dead son home by ship—
Eteoclus, who fell to the Theban spear—
and to seek my daughter, wife of Capaneus,
who sped from my house in longing to die with her husband.
Before this, she was watched at home; beset
by present troubles, I dismissed the guards;
and she has gone. I think she must be here;
if you have seen her, tell me.

EVADNE

Why ask them?

I am here on a rock above his pyre, my father—
lightly poised, like a bird, for a flight of doom.

IPHIS

My child, what wind has blown you here? What errand?
Why did you slip from home and come to this land?

EVADNE

You would be angry if I told my plans;
I do not wish you to hear about them, father.

IPHIS

What? Is it not right that your father should know?

EVADNE

You would not be an able judge of my intent.

IPHIS

For whom have you put on this finery?

EVADNE

My dress has glory in its meaning, father.

IPHIS

You don't look like one in mourning for her husband.

EVADNE

No, I have made myself ready for something new.

IPHIS

And yet you appear beside his tomb and pyre?

EVADNE

I come to celebrate a victory.

IPHIS

I beg you, tell me over whom you won it.

EVADNE

Over all women on whom the sun looks down.

IPHIS

In Athena's skills, or in the ways of prudence?

EVADNE

In valor: I shall lie with my husband in death.

IPHIS

You speak in sickly riddles. What is this?

EVADNE

I rush to the pyre of fallen Capaneus.

IPHIS

My daughter! Do not speak such words in public.

EVADNE

I want it known by everyone in Argos.

IPHIS

I shall not suffer you to do this thing.

EVADNE

No matter; I am beyond the reach of your hand.
My body falls! a flight not dear to you
but to me and the husband who will burn with me.

(Exit Evadne leaping down into the pyre.)

CHORUS [*singing, while Iphis speaks in reply*]

Woman! Terrible the deed you brought to pass!

IPHIS

Daughters of Argos! I am ruined, doomed.

CHORUS

Having borne this heavy woe,
ah! can you bear to see
her wildly daring deed?

IPHIS

The world holds no more miserable man.

CHORUS

What suffering is yours! A part of Oedipus' doom
has befallen you, old sire, and my poor city.

IPHIS

In grief I ask: Why cannot mortals be
twice young, then reach old age a second time?
If anything goes wrong at home, we right it
by afterthoughts; but not so with a life.
If youth and age came twice, a double life
would be our lot, and we could set things right
no matter what mistakes we'd made. When I saw others
with families, I became an adorer of children
and sorely longed for some to call my own.
If I had come to this experience
with children, and known what it is for a father to lose them,
never would I have reached the point of woe
where now I stand: having brought into the world°
a noble youth, then to be robbed of him.
And now, in my wretchedness, what shall I do?
Return to my house, to see the emptiness
of many rooms, and a hopeless round of living?
Or shall I go where Capaneus once dwelt?
What a delight that was, when I had my daughter!
But now she is no more—she who would draw
my cheek to her lips and clasp my head in her hands.
To an old father, nothing is more sweet
than a daughter. Boys are more spirited, but their ways
are not so tender. Quickly, take me home
and give me to the dark, to starve until
my aged frame is wasted and I die.
What will I gain by touching my child's bones?
  O harsh old age! How loathsome is your grip!
How I hate those who want to stretch life out,
counting on meats and drinks and magic spells
to turn the stream aside and stave off death.

They're useless to the world, they ought to die:
away with them! Let them leave it to the young.

(Exit Iphis to one side. Enter from the other side Theseus, and the sons of the Seven carrying urns containing their ashes.)

CHORUS [*chanting*]

Look, look! Alas! They are bringing
the bones of my children who perished.
Attendants, take hold of a weak old woman.
Grief for my children has robbed me of my strength.
I have been alive for many lengths of time
and many woes have made me melt in tears.
What greater pain can mortals feel than this:
to see their children dead before their eyes?

BOYS° [*singing, with the Chorus singing in reply*]

STROPHE A

Sorrowful mothers! Out of the fire
I bring, I bring my father's limbs;
a weight not weightless, so great is my grief
as I gather my all in a little space.

CHORUS

Ah, ah! Why do you bring
tears for the mother whom the fallen loved?
A little heap of dust instead of bodies
once glorious in Mycenae?

BOYS

ANTISTROPHE A

You are childless! childless! and I,
having lost my unhappy father, will dwell
an orphan in a house of loss,
cut off from the man who gave me life.

CHORUS

Ah, ah! Where is the labor
spent on my children? Where, the reward of childbirth,

a mother's care, sleepless devotion of eyes,
the loving kiss on the face?

BOYS

STROPHE B

They have gone, they are no more. Oh, my father!
They have gone.

CHORUS

The air holds them now,
crumbled to dust in the fire;
they have winged their way to Hades.

BOYS

Father, I beg you, hear your children's cries!°
Shall I ever set my shield against your foes,
making your murder engender death? May that day come!

BOYS

ANTISTROPHE B

If a god is willing, justice will be done
for our fathers.

CHORUS

This evil sleeps not yet.
It grieves me. I have had enough
ill chance, enough of woe.

BOYS

Some day Asopus' gleam will welcome me
as I march in the bronze armor of Danaus' sons
on a campaign to demand revenge for my fallen father.

BOYS

STROPHE C

Still I seem to see you, father, before my eyes . . .

CHORUS

. . . planting your kiss, so loved, upon my cheek.

BOYS

But your encouraging words
are borne away on the air.

CHORUS

He left woe to us both: his mother,
and you, whom grief for your father will never leave.

BOYS

ANTISTROPHE C

I bear so great a burden that it has destroyed me.

CHORUS

Come, let me lay the dear dust close to my breast.

BOYS

Oh, piteous words! I weep
to hear them; they pierce my heart.

CHORUS

Child, you have gone: never again
shall I see you, darling of your beloved mother.

THESEUS

Adrastus! Women born of Argive families!
You see these boys, holding in their hands
the bodies of their fathers, noble men
whom I took up for burial. To them
I and the city now present the ashes.
You, who see now what you have gained from me,
must keep this act in grateful recollection,
and tell your children constantly to honor
this city, handing down from son to son
the memory of answered prayers. Zeus
and the gods in heaven know the kindnesses
of which we thought you worthy. Go in peace.

ADRASTUS

Theseus, we are aware of all the good

you have done the land of Argos, in its need
of benefactors, and our gratitude
will never fade. We've been nobly treated by you,
and we owe you noble actions in return.

THESEUS
How can I be of further service to you?

ADRASTUS
By faring well, as you and your city deserve.

THESEUS
We shall; and may you have the same good fortune.

(Athena appears from above.)

ATHENA
Theseus, hear what I, Athena, tell you.
There is a duty that you must perform
to help the city now. Do not entrust
these bones to the boys, to take to the land of Argos,
releasing them so lightly. First exact
an oath, in compensation for the efforts
you and the city have made. Adrastus here
must swear—he has authority, as king,
to take an oath on behalf of all the land
of Danaus' sons. And this shall be the oath:
"Argos will never bring against this country
its armed forces in war. And if others try
to invade it, she will resist them by arms."
But if they break their oath and attack, then pray
that the Argive land may fall again to ruin.
Now hear me name the vessel for the blood
from the sacrifice you must perform. You have
inside your house a tripod with feet of bronze.
After destroying Ilium's foundations
long years ago, Heracles, going forth
on another labor, told you to set that vessel

on the altar of Apollo. Over it
you must cut the throats of three sheep, and inscribe
the oath on the hollow of the tripod; then
present it to the god who has charge of Delphi,
to be preserved in memory of the oath
and as witness to it in the eyes of Hellas.
The sharp-edged knife, with which you will perform
the sacrifice and deal the death-wound, you must bury
deep in the earth, here, beside the seven
pyres of the fallen. Then, if the Argives ever
attack the city, the knife, displayed, will work
fear in their hearts, and an evil journey home.
After all this is done, then escort the dead from the land,
and dedicate a shrine to the god beside
the crossroad to the Isthmus, where the bodies
were purified by fire.
These are my words
to you. To the sons of the Argives, I proclaim:
when you are men you will sack Ismenus' city,
avenging the murder of your fallen fathers.
You, Aegialeus, will take your father's place
as a young commander, and you, the son of Tydeus
from Aetolia, named Diomedes by your father.
No sooner shall you get your beards than you'll march
a mighty force of bronze-clad Danaans
against the Thebans' seven-mouthed walls. Your coming
will bring them sorrow—lion cubs you are,
true-bred sackers of cities! This shall befall:
you'll be known through Greece as the Successors of the Seven,
a theme of future song. So great will be
your expedition, favored by the gods.

THESEUS

I shall obey your orders, Queen Athena!
You have corrected me; I won't go wrong again.
Now I shall bind this man to me by oath.

Only, I pray you, set me in the right path;
so long as you mean kindly to the city,
our life will be secure to the end of time.

(*Exit Athena.*)

CHORUS [*chanting*]
Now let us go, Adrastus, and give our word
to this man and his city, whose deeds for us
deserve the highest honors we can give.

(*Exit all.*)

ELECTRA

Translated by EMILY TOWNSEND VERMEULE

ELECTRA: INTRODUCTION

The Play: Date and Composition

There is no external evidence available for determining when Euripides' *Electra* was first produced. The play used to be dated to 413 BCE on the basis of a presumed allusion near its end to an episode in Athens' expedition against Sicily in that year, but more recently scholars have grown wary of this kind of argument and prefer to use the play's meter to date it, which would place it around 420 BCE. Presumably Euripides wrote it for the annual competition at the Great Dionysian Festival in Athens. What the other three plays were in Euripides' tetralogy of that year, and how they fared in the competition, are unknown.

The Myth

Electra presents an episode from the tragic vicissitudes of the house of the Pelopids, the royal dynasty of Argos (or Mycenae): Agamemnon, his wife Clytemnestra, her lover Aegisthus, and her children Iphigenia, Electra, and Orestes. After Agamemnon returned from Troy, Clytemnestra and Aegisthus murdered him. The action of Euripides' play begins some years later. Aegisthus and Clytemnestra are still in power; Orestes has been hiding in exile; in what is surely a surprising Euripidean innovation, Electra has been married off to a local farmer to ensure that she will not bear children of high enough status to avenge her father's murder. After the beginning of the play introduces us to Electra and the farmer, Orestes returns from exile with his companion Pylades and is recognized by Electra. By the play's end, with the help of his sister, Orestes has succeeded in killing first Aegisthus, then their mother, Clytemnestra.

Euripides' *Electra* dramatizes one of the most popular stories in all of Greek tragedy. Euripides himself returned repeatedly to this mythic complex to treat other episodes from it, in *Iphigenia among the Taurians* (written ca. 414 BCE), *Orestes* (produced 408 BCE), and *Iphigenia in Aulis* (produced posthumously after 406 BCE). The same events that serve as the basis for Euripides' play also formed the subject of Aeschylus' surviving trilogy the *Oresteia*—it is its second play, *The Libation Bearers*, that bears closest comparison to Euripides' *Electra*—and Euripides' tragedy seems to make a number of obvious references, some of them apparently quite polemical, to Aeschylus' version. Furthermore, Sophocles dealt with exactly the same material in his *Electra*, which has also survived but cannot be dated precisely. There are evident similarities and no less evident differences between Sophocles' and Euripides' plays, and for centuries scholars have argued inconclusively about which play preceded—and may have influenced—the other. But only internal evidence is available, and it is slight and slippery. The question remains open.

Transmission and Reception

Electra was not one of Euripides' most popular plays in antiquity, in contrast to his enormously popular *Orestes*, but it has become increasingly influential in recent years, especially because of its obvious allusions and contrasts to Aeschylus' *Oresteia*. It survived antiquity only by the accident of being among the so-called "alphabetic plays" (see "Introduction to Euripides" in this volume, p. 3). Like the others in this group, it comes down to us only by a single manuscript in rather poor condition (and by its copies) and it is not accompanied by the ancient commentaries (scholia) that explain various kinds of interpretative difficulties. Further evidence that it was not very popular in antiquity is that only two papyri bearing parts of its text have been discovered. The play has left little or no trace in ancient pictorial art.

While the story of Orestes' vengeance on Clytemnestra and Aegisthus has never ceased to fascinate authors and audiences in all literary genres and other media, it is hard to find clear cases in which it is specifically Euripides' tragedy—rather than Aeschylus' or Sophocles'—that has influenced a later version. Since the Renaissance it has tended to be Sophocles' tragedy, or, especially since the nineteenth century, Aeschylus' trilogy, that has been preferred. Some of the few twentieth-century texts that display the direct influence of Euripides' tragedy are Maurice Baring's play *After Euripides' "Electra"* (1911), Robinson Jeffers' dramatic poem *The Tower beyond Tragedy* (1926, adapted for the stage 1950), Richard Aldington's poem "Troy's Down" (1943), Michael Cacoyannis' film *Elektra* with Irene Papas and music by Mikis Theodorakis (1962), Hugo Claus' tragedy *Orestes* (1976), and Suzuki Tadashi's Japanese adaptation *Clytemnestra* (1980).

ELECTRA

Characters

FARMER, married to Electra
ELECTRA, daughter of Agamemnon and Clytemnestra
ORESTES, son of Agamemnon and Clytemnestra
PYLADES, a friend of Orestes (nonspeaking)
CHORUS of Argive peasant women
OLD MAN
MESSENGER, a servant of Orestes
CLYTEMNESTRA, widow of Agamemnon, mother of Electra and Orestes
CASTOR and POLYDEUCES (the Dioscuri), Clytemnestra's brothers

Scene: In front of the Farmer's cottage in the countryside near Argos; before the house stands an altar to Apollo.

FARMER

Argos, old bright floor of the world,° Inachus' pouring
tides—King Agamemnon once on a thousand ships
hoisted the war god here and sailed across to Troy.
He killed the monarch of the land of Ilium,
Priam; he sacked the glorious city of Dardanus;
he came home to Argos here and high on the towering
shrines
nailed up the massive loot of Barbary for the gods.
So, over there he did well. But in his own house

he died in ambush planned for him by his own wife
Clytemnestra and by her lover Aegisthus' hand.
He lost the ancient scepter of Tantalus; he is dead.
Thyestes' son Aegisthus walks king in the land
and keeps the dead man's wife for himself, Tyndareus' child.
As for the children he left home when he sailed to Troy,
his son Orestes and his flowering girl Electra,
Orestes almost died under Aegisthus' fist,
but his father's ancient servant snatched the boy away,
gave him to Strophius to bring up in the land of Phocis.
Electra kept on waiting within her father's house.
But when the burning season of young ripeness took her,
then the great princes of the land of Greece came begging
her bridal. Aegisthus was afraid—afraid her son
if noble in blood would punish Agamemnon's death.
He held her in the house sundered from every love.
Yet, even guarded so, she filled his nights with fear
lest she in secret to some prince might still bear sons;
he laid his plans to kill her. But her mother, though
savage in soul, then saved her from Aegisthus' hand.
The lady had excuse for murdering her husband
but flinched from killing a child, afraid of the world's ill will.
So then Aegisthus framed a new design. He swore
to any man who captured Agamemnon's son
running in exile and murdered him, a price of gold.
Electra—he gave her to me as a gift, to hold
her as my wife.
Now, I was born of Mycenaean
family, on this ground I have nothing to be ashamed of,
in breeding I shine bright enough. But in my fortune
I rank as a pauper, which blots out all decent blood.
He gave her to me, a weak man, to weaken his own fear,
for if a man of high position had taken her
he might have roused awake the sleeping Agamemnon's
blood—justice might have knocked at Aegisthus' door.
I have not touched her and the love god Cypris knows it:

I never shamed the girl in bed, she is still virgin.
I would feel ugly taking the daughter of a wealthy man
and violating her. I was not bred to such an honor.
And poor laboring Orestes, my brother-in-law in name—
I suffer his grief, I think his thoughts, if he came home
to Argos and saw his sister so unlucky in her wedding.
Whoever says that I am a born fool to keep
a young girl in my house and never touch her body,
I say he measures wisdom by a crooked line
of morals. He should know he's as great a fool as I.

(Enter Electra from the house, carrying a water jar on her head.)

ELECTRA

O night, black night, whose breast nurses the golden stars,
I wander through your darkness, head lifted to bear
this pot I carry to the sources of the river—
I do not need to, I chose this slavery myself
to demonstrate to the gods Aegisthus' outrageousness—
and cry my pain to Father in the great bright air.
For my own mother, she, Tyndareus' deadly daughter,
has thrown me out like dirt from the house, to her husband's joy,
and while she breeds new children in Aegisthus' bed
has made me and Orestes mere appendages to the house.

FARMER

Now why, unhappy girl, must you for my sake wrestle
such heavy work though you were raised in comfort?
Although I tell you often to stop, you just refuse.

ELECTRA

I think you equal to the gods in kindliness:
for you've never taken advantage of me though I'm in trouble.
It's great fortune for people to find a kind physician
of suffering, which I have found in finding you.
Indeed without your bidding I should make your labor

as light as I have strength for; you will bear it better
if I claim some share with you in the work. Outdoors
you have enough to do; my place is in the house,
to keep it tidy. When a man comes in from work
it is nice to find his hearthplace looking swept and clean.

FARMER

Well, if your heart is set on helping, go. The spring
is not so distant from the house. At light of dawn
I will put the cows to pasture and start planting the fields.
A lazy man may rustle gods upon his tongue
but never makes a living if he will not work.

(Exit Farmer and Electra to the side. Enter Orestes and Pylades from the other side, with attendants.)

ORESTES

Pylades, I consider you the first of men
in loyalty and love to me, my host and friend.
You only of my friends gave honor and respect
to me, Orestes, suffering as I suffer from Aegisthus.
He killed my father—he and my destructive mother.
I come from secret converse with the holy god
to this outpost of Argos—no one knows I am here—
to counterchange my father's death for death to his killers.
During the night just passed I found my father's tomb,
gave him my tears in gift and sheared my hair in mourning,
and sprinkled ceremonial sheep's blood on the fire,
holding these rites concealed from the tyrants who rule here.
   I will not set my foot inside the city walls.
I chose this gatepost of the land deliberately,
compacting a double purpose. First, if any lookout
should recognize me I can run for foreign soil;
second, to find my sister. For they say she married
and, tamed to domestic love, lives here no longer virgin.
I want to be with her and take her as my partner
in killing, and learn more about things inside the city.

And now, since lady dawn is lifting her white face,
let's come away from the path on which we have been
treading.
Perhaps a field-bound farmer or some serving woman
will meet us on the road, and we can ask discreetly
whether my sister lives anywhere in this place.
Quick now! I see some sort of serving girl approach
with a jar of fountain water on her close-cropped head—
it looks heavy for her. Let's sit here, let us listen
to the slave girl. Pylades, perhaps at last we shall hear
the news we hoped for when we crossed into this land.

(They hide behind the altar. Enter Electra from the side.)

ELECTRA [*singing*]

STROPHE A

Quicken the foot's rush—time has struck—O
walk now, walk now weeping aloud,
O for my grief!
I was bred Agamemnon's child,
formed in the flesh of Clytemnestra,
Tyndareus' hellish daughter,
Argos' people have named me true:
wretched Electra.
Cry, cry for my toil and pain,
cry for the hatred of living.
Father who in the halls of death
lie hacked by your wife and Aegisthus, O
Agamemnon!

MESODE A

Come, waken the mourning again,
rouse up for me the sweetness of tears.

ANTISTROPHE A

Quicken the foot's rush—time has struck—
walk now, walk now weeping aloud,
O for my grief!

In what city and in what house, O
brother of grief, do you wander in exile?°
You left me locked in the cursed
palace chambers for doom to strike
your sister in sorrow.
Come, loose me from miseries, come
save me, pitiful me—O Zeus,
Zeus!—to help avenge our father's hate-spilled blood,
steering your exiled foot to land
in Argos.

STROPHE B

Set this vessel down from my head, O
take it, while I lift music of mourning
by night to my father.
Father, the maenad song of death°
I cry you among the dead
beneath the earth, the words I pour
day after day unending
as I move, ripping my throat with sharp
nails, fists pounding my shorn
head for your dying.

MESODE B

Ai, ai, strike my head!
I, like the swan of echoing song
in descant note at the water's edge
who calls to its father so dearly loved
but dead now in the hidden net
of twisted meshes, mourn you thus
in agony dying, father,

ANTISTROPHE B

body steeped in the final bath,
rest most pitiful, sleep of death.
O for my grief!
Bitter the axe and bitter the gash,

bitter the road you walked°
from Troy straight to their plotted net—
your lady did not receive you
with victor's ribbons or flowers to crown you,
but with double-edged steel she made you
savage sport for Aegisthus, and won
herself a shifty lover.

(Enter the Chorus of Argive peasant women from the side.)

CHORUS [*singing in a lyric interchange with Electra, who continues to sing*]

STROPHE

Princess, daughter of Agamemnon,
we have come to your country dwelling,
Electra, to see you.
There came, came a man
bred on the milk of the hills,
a Mycenaean mountaineer
who gave me word that two days from now
the Argives proclaim at large
a holy feast, when all the maidens
will pass in procession up to the temple of Hera.

ELECTRA

Dear friends, not for festivities,
not for twisted bracelets of gold
does my heart take wing in delight.
I am too sad, I cannot stand
in choral joy with the maidens of Argos
or beat the tune with my whirling foot;
rather with tears by night
and tears by day I fill my soul
shaking in grief and fear.
Look! Think! Would my filthy hair
and robe all torn into slavish rags
do public honor to Agamemnon's

daughter, the princess?
Honor to Troy which will never forget
my conquering father?

CHORUS

ANTISTROPHE

Great, great is the goddess. Come,
I will lend you a dress to wear,
thick-woven of wool,
and gold—be gracious, accept—
gold for holiday glitter.
Do you think your tears and refusing
honor to the gods will ever hurt
your haters? Not by sounding lament
but only by prayer and reverent love
for the gods, my child, will you have gentler days.

ELECTRA

Gods? Not one god has heard
my helpless cry or watched of old
over my murdered father.
Mourn again for the wasted dead,
mourn for the living outlaw
somewhere prisoned in foreign lands
passing from one laborer's hearth to the next
though born of a glorious sire.
And I! I in a peasant's hut
waste my life like melting wax,
exiled and barred from my father's home
to a scarred mountain field,
while my mother rolls in her bloody bed
and plays at love with another man.

CHORUS LEADER [*speaking*]

Yes, like Helen, your mother's sister—charged and found
guilty of massive pain by Greece and by your house.

(Orestes and Pylades appear from behind the altar.)

ELECTRA [*now speaking*]

Oh, oh! women, I break off my death-bound cry.
Look! there are strangers here close to the house who crouch
huddled beside the altar and rise up in ambush.
Run, you take the path, and I into the house
with one swift rush can still escape these criminals.

ORESTES

Poor girl, stand still, and fear not. I would never hurt you.

ELECTRA

Phoebus Apollo, help! I kneel to you. Do not kill me.

ORESTES

I hope I shall kill others hated more than you.

ELECTRA

Go away; don't touch. You have no right to touch my body.

ORESTES

There is no person I could touch with greater right.

ELECTRA

Why were you hiding, sword in hand, so near my house?

ORESTES

Stand still and listen. You will agree I have rights here.

ELECTRA

I stand here utterly in your power. You are stronger.

ORESTES

I have come to bring you a spoken message from your brother.

ELECTRA

Dearest of strangers, is he alive or is he dead?

ORESTES

Alive. I wish to give you all the good news first.

ELECTRA

God bless your days, as you deserve for such sweet words.

ORESTES

I share your gift with you that we may both be blessed.

ELECTRA

Where is he now, attempting to bear unbearable exile?

ORESTES

He is wrecked, and is included in no city's laws.

ELECTRA

Tell me, he is not poor? not hungry for daily bread?

ORESTES

He has bread, yet he has the exile's constant hunger.

ELECTRA

You came to bring a message—what are his words for me?

ORESTES

"Are you alive? And if you are, what is your life?"

ELECTRA

I think you see me. First, my body wasted and dry.

ORESTES

Yes, sadness has wasted you so greatly I could weep.

ELECTRA

Next, my head razor-cropped like a victim of the Scythians.

ORESTES

Your brother's life and father's death both bite at your heart.

ELECTRA

Alas, there's nothing else that I love more than them.

ORESTES

You grieve me. Whom do you think your brother loves
but you?

ELECTRA

He is not here. He loves me, but he is not here.

ORESTES

Why do you live in a place like this, so far from town?

ELECTRA

Because I married, stranger—a wedding much like death.

ORESTES

Bad news for your brother. Your husband is a Mycenaean?

ELECTRA

But not the man my father would have wished me to marry.

ORESTES

Tell me. I am listening, I can say it to your brother.

ELECTRA

This is his house. I live quite isolated here.

ORESTES

A ditchdigger, a cowherd would look well living here.

ELECTRA

He is a poor man but well born, and he respects me.

ORESTES

Respects? What does your husband understand by "respect"?

ELECTRA

He has never been violent or touched me in my bed.

ORESTES

A vow of chastity? or he finds you unattractive?

ELECTRA

He finds it attractive not to insult my royal blood.

ORESTES

How could he not be pleased at marrying so well?

ELECTRA

He judges the man who gave me had no right to, stranger.

ORESTES

I see—afraid Orestes might avenge your honor.

ELECTRA

Afraid of that, yes—he is also decent by nature.

ORESTES

Ah.
You paint one of nature's gentlemen. We must treat him well.

ELECTRA

We will, if my absent brother ever gets home again.

ORESTES

Your mother took the wedding calmly, I suppose?

ELECTRA

Women save all their love for their men, not for their children.

ORESTES

What was in Aegisthus' mind, to insult you so?

ELECTRA

He hoped that I, so wedded, would have worthless sons.

ORESTES

Too weak for undertaking blood-revenge on him?

ELECTRA

That was his hope. I hope to make him pay for it.

ORESTES

This husband of your mother's—does he know you are virgin?

ELECTRA

No, he knows nothing. We have played our parts in silence.

ORESTES

These women listening as we talk are friends of yours?

ELECTRA

Good enough friends to keep what we say well concealed.

ORESTES
How should Orestes play his part, if he comes to Argos?

ELECTRA
If he comes? Ugly talk. The time has long been ripe.

ORESTES
Say he comes; still how could he kill his father's killers?

ELECTRA
By being just as daring as once his enemies were.°

ORESTES
To kill your mother with his help—could you do that?

ELECTRA
Yes, with the very same axe that cut Father to ruin.

ORESTES
May I tell him what you say and how determined you are?

ELECTRA
Tell him how gladly I would die in Mother's blood.

ORESTES
O, I wish Orestes could stand here and listen.

ELECTRA
Yet if I saw him I should hardly know him, sir.

ORESTES
No wonder. You were both very young when you were parted.

ELECTRA
I have only one friend who might still know his face.

ORESTES
The man who saved him once from death, as the story goes?

ELECTRA
Yes, very old now—he was my father's tutor.

ORESTES

When your father died did his body find some burial?

ELECTRA

He found what he found. He was thrown on the dirt
outdoors.

ORESTES

I cannot bear it. What have you said? Even a stranger's
pain bites strangely deep and hurts us when we hear it.
Tell me the rest, and with new knowledge I will bring
Orestes your tale, so harsh to hear but so imperative
to be heard. Uneducated men are pitiless,
but we who are educated pity much. And we pay
a high price for being intelligent. Wisdom hurts.

CHORUS LEADER

The same excitement stirs my mind in this as his—
I live far from the city and I know its troubles
hardly at all. Now I would like to learn them too.

ELECTRA

I will tell if I must—and must tell you as my friend—
how my luck, and my father's, is too heavy to lift.
Since you have moved me to speak so, stranger, I must beg
that you will tell Orestes all my distress, and his.
First tell him how I am kept like a beast in stable rags,
my skin heavy with grease and dirt. Describe to him
this hut—my home, who used to live in the king's palace.
I weave my clothes myself and slavelike at the loom
must work or else walk naked through the world in nothing.
I fetch and carry water from the riverside,
I am deprived of holy festivals and dances,
I can't spend time with women since I am a girl,°
I can't spend time with Castor, who is close in blood
and was my suitor, before he rose to join the gods.
My mother in the glory of her Phrygian loot

sits on the throne, while circled at her feet the girls
of Asia stoop, whom Father won at the sack of Troy,
their clothes woven in snowy wool from Ida, pinned
with golden brooches, while the walls and floor are stained
still with my father's black and rotting blood. The man
who murdered him goes riding grand in Father's chariot,
with bloody hands and high delight lifting the staff
of office by which Father marshaled the Greek army.
The tomb of Agamemnon finds no honor yet,
never yet drenched with holy liquids or made green
in myrtle branches, barren of bright sacrifice.
But in his drunken fits, my mother's lover, brilliant
man, triumphant leaps and dances on the mound
and pelts my father's stone memorial with rocks
and dares to shout against us with his boldened tongue:
"Where is your son Orestes? When will that noble youth
come to protect your tomb?" Insults to an absent man.
Kind stranger, as I ask you, tell him all these things.
For many call him home again— and I speak for them,
all of them, with my hands and tongue and grieving mind
and head, shaven in mourning; and his father calls too.
All will be shamed if he whose father captured Troy
cannot in single courage kill a single man,
although his strength is younger and his birth more noble.

CHORUS LEADER

Electra! I can see your husband on the road.
He has finished his field work and is coming home.

(The Farmer enters from the side.)

FARMER

Hey there! Who are these strangers standing at our gates?
What is the errand that could bring them to our distant
courtyard? Are they demanding something from me? A nice
woman should never stand in gossip with young men.

ELECTRA

My dearest husband, do not come suspecting me.
You shall hear their story, the whole truth. They come
as messengers to me with tidings of Orestes.
Strangers, I ask you to forgive him what he said.

FARMER

What news? Is Orestes still alive in the bright light?

ELECTRA

So they have told me, and I do not doubt their words.

FARMER

Does he still remember his father's troubles, and yours?

ELECTRA

We hope so. But an exile is a helpless man.

FARMER

Then what is this message of his? What have they come to tell?

ELECTRA

He sent them simply to see my troubles for themselves.

FARMER

What they don't see themselves I imagine you have told them.

ELECTRA

They know it all. I took good care that they missed nothing.

FARMER

Why were our doors not opened to them long ago?
Come into the house, you will find entertainment
to answer your good news, such as my roof can offer.
Servants, pick up their baggage, bring it all indoors.
Come, no polite refusals. You are here as friends
most dear to me who meet you now. Though I am poor
in money, I think you will not find our manners poor.

ORESTES

By the gods! Is this the man who helps you fake a marriage,
the one who does not wish to cast shame on Orestes?

ELECTRA

This is the man they know as poor Electra's husband.

ORESTES

Alas,
we try to find good men and cannot recognize them
when met, since all our human heritage runs mongrel.
At times I have seen descendants of the noblest family
quite worthless, while poor fathers had outstanding sons;
inside the souls of wealthy men bleak famine lives
while minds of stature struggle trapped in starving bodies.
How then can man distinguish man, what test can he use?°
The test of wealth? That measure means poverty of mind.
Of poverty? The pauper owns one thing, the sickness
of his condition, a compelling teacher of evil.
By nerve in war? Yet who, when a spear is aimed right at
his face, will stand to witness his companion's courage?
We might as well just toss these matters to the winds.
This fellow here is no great man among the Argives,
not dignified by family in the eyes of the world—
he is a face in the crowd, and yet I choose him champion.
Can you not come to understand, you empty-minded,
opinion-stuffed people, to judge a man by how
he lives with others: manners are nobility's touchstone?
Such men of manners can control our cities best,°
and homes, but the wellborn sportsman, long on muscle,
short
on brains, is only good for a statue in the park—
not even sterner in the shocks of war than weaker
men, for courage is the gift of character.
Now let us take whatever rest this house can give;
this man here, Agamemnon's child, the absent man
for whom I've come, deserves no less. We should go now

indoors, servants, inside the house, since a poor host
who's eager to entertain is better than a rich one.
I do praise and accept his most kind reception
but would have been more pleased if your brother on the
crest
of fortune could have brought me into a fortunate house.
Perhaps he may still come; Apollo's oracles
are strong, though human prophecy is best ignored.

(Exit Orestes and Pylades into the house with their attendants.)

CHORUS LEADER

Now more than ever in our lives, Electra, joy
makes our hearts light and warm. Perhaps now fortune, first
running such painful steps, will stand on firmer footing.

ELECTRA *(To the farmer.)*

You thoughtless man! You know quite well the house is bare;
why take these strangers in? They are better born than you.

FARMER

Why? Because if they are the gentlemen they seem,
will they not be content with small things as with great?

ELECTRA

Small is the word for you. Now the mistake is made,
go quickly to my father's loved and ancient servant
who by Tanaus river, where it cuts the land
of Argos off from Spartan country, goes his rounds
watching his flocks in distant exile from the town.
Tell him these strangers have descended on me;° ask
him to come and bring some food fit for distinguished
guests.
He will surely be happy; he will bless the gods
when he hears the child he saved so long ago still lives.
Besides, we cannot get help from the family house,
from Mother—our news would fly to her on bitter wings,
cruel as she is, if she should hear Orestes lives.

FARMER

Well, if you wish it, I can pass your message on
to the old man. But you get quick into the house
and ready up what's there. A woman when she has to
can always find some food to set a decent table.
The house holds little, yet it is enough, I know,
to keep these strangers full of food at least one day.

(Exit Electra into the house.)

When things like this occur, my intellect reflects.
I contemplate the mighty power found in money:
money you can spend on guests; money you can pay the
    doctor
when you get sick. But little difference does money make
for our daily bread, and when a man has eaten that,
the rich man and the poor one hold just the same amount.

(Exit the Farmer to the side.)

CHORUS [*singing*]

STROPHE A

O glorious ships that sailed across to Troy once
    moving on infinite wooden oars
    attending the circling chorus of Nereid dancers
where the dolphin delighting in the pipe-
    melody all about the sea-
    blue prows went plunging;
you led the goddess Thetis' son,
light-striding Achilles, on his way
with Agamemnon to Ilium's cliffs
    where Simois pours into the sea.

ANTISTROPHE A

The Nereids passed Euboea's headlands
    bringing the heavy shield of gold,
forged on Hephaestus' anvil, and golden armor.
Up Mount Pelion, up the jut

of Ossa's holy slopes on high,
up the nymphs' spy-rocks
they hunted the aged horseman's hill
where he trained the boy as a dawn for Greece,
the son of Thetis, sea-bred and swift-
footed for the sons of Atreus.

STROPHE B

Once I heard from a man out of Troy, known to the port
in Nauplia close to Argos,
of your brilliant shield, O goddess'
child, how in its circled space
these signs, scenes, were in blazon warning,
terrors for Phrygia:
running in frieze on its massive rim,
Perseus lifting the severed head
of the Gorgon, cut at the neck;°
he walks on wings over the sea;
Hermes is with him, messenger of Zeus,
great Maia's
child of the flocks and forests.

ANTISTROPHE B

Out of the shield's curved center glittered afar the high
shining round of the sun
driving with wingèd horses,
and the chorused stars of upper air—
Pleiades, Hyades—Hector eyed them,
and swerved to flight.
Over the helmet of beaten gold
Sphinxes snatch in hooking nails
their prey trapped with song. On the hollow
greave, the lioness' fire breath
flares in her clawed track as she runs,
staring
at the wind-borne foal of Peirene.

EPODE

All along the blade of the deadly sword, hooves pounding,
horses leapt; black above their backs the dust blew.
But the lord of such spearmen
you killed by lust of sex and sin
of mind, daughter of Tyndareus.
For this the sons of heaven will send
you a judgment of death;° some far
day I shall still see your blood fall
red from your neck by the iron sword.

(Enter the Old Man from the side, carrying provisions for a feast.)

OLD MAN

Where is my young mistress and my lady queen,
the child of Agamemnon, whom I raised and loved?
How steep this house seems set to me, with rough approach,
as I grow old for climbing on these withered legs.
But when your friends call, you must come and drag along
and hump your spine till it snaps and bend your knees like pins.

(Enter Electra from the house.)

Why there she is—my daughter, look at you by the door!
I am here. I have brought you from my cropping sheep
a newborn lamb, a tender one, just pulled from the teat,
and flowers looped in garlands, cheese white from the churn,
and this stored treasure of the wine god, aged and fragrant—
not much of it, I know, but sweet, and very good
to pour into the cup with other, weaker wine.
Let someone take this all in to the guests indoors,
for I have cried a little and would like to dry
my face and eyes out here on my cloak—more holes than wool.

(A servant does as instructed.)

ELECTRA

Old man, please tell me, why is your face so stained with tears?
After so long has my grief stirred your thoughts again,
or is it poor Orestes in his cheerless exile
you mourn for, or my father, whom your two old hands
once raised and helped without reward for self or loved ones?

OLD MAN

Reward, no. Yet I could not stop myself, in this:
for I came past his tomb, circling from the road,
and fell to the earth there, weeping for him, alone,
and opening this winesack intended for your guests
I poured libation, and I wreathed the stone in myrtle.
And there I saw on the burning-altar a black-fleeced
sheep, throat cut and blood still warm in its dark stream,
and curling locks of bright blond hair cut off in gift.
I stopped, quiet, to wonder, child, what man had courage
to visit at that tomb. It could not be an Argive.
Is there a chance your brother has arrived in secret
and paused to wonder at his father's shabby tomb?
Look at the lock of hair, match it to your own head,
see if it is not exactly twin to yours in color.
Often a father's blood, running in separate veins,
makes siblings' bodies almost mirrors in their form.

ELECTRA

Old man, I always thought you were wiser than you sound
if you really think my brother, who is brave and bold,
would come to our land in hiding, frightened by Aegisthus!
Besides, how could a lock of his hair match with mine?
one from a man with rugged training in the ring
and games, one combed and girlish? It is not possible.
Besides, you could find many matching curls of many people
not bred in the same house, old man, nor matched in blood.

OLD MAN

At least go set your foot in the print of his hunting boot
and see if it is not the same as yours, my child.

ELECTRA

But how could rocky ground possibly receive
the imprint of a foot? And if it could be traced,
it would not be the same for brother and for sister,
a man's foot and a girl's—of course his would be bigger.

OLD MAN

Is there no piece then, if your brother should come home,°
of weaving, that loom pattern by which you would know the cloth
you wove and I wrapped him in, to rescue him from death?

ELECTRA

You know quite well that when Orestes left for exile
I was still very small. And even if a child's hand
could weave, how could a grown man still wear those boy's clothes
unless his shirt and tunic lengthened with his body?
Some pitying stranger must have passed the tomb and cut
a mourning lock, or townsmen slipping past the lookouts.°

OLD MAN

Where are the strangers now? I want to look them over
and draw them out with conversation of your brother.

(Enter Orestes and Pylades from the house.)

ELECTRA

Here they come striding lightly from the cottage now.

OLD MAN

Well. They look highborn enough, but the coin may prove
false. Often a noble face hides filthy ways.
Nevertheless—
Greetings, strangers, I wish you well.

ORESTES

And greetings in return, old sir.
Electra, tell me,
to what friends of yours does this human antique belong?

ELECTRA

This is the man who raised and loved my father, sir.

ORESTES

What! the one who saved your brother once from death?

ELECTRA

Indeed he saved him—if indeed he still is safe.

ORESTES

Ah, so!
Why does he stare upon me like a man who squints
at the bright stamp on silver? Do I look like somebody?

ELECTRA

Perhaps he's just happy seeing someone of Orestes' age.

ORESTES

Dear Orestes. Why does he walk round me in circles?

ELECTRA

Stranger, I am astonished too as I look at him.

OLD MAN

Mistress, now pray. Daughter Electra, pray to the gods.

ELECTRA

For which of the things I have, or which that I don't have?

OLD MAN

For a treasure of love within your grasp, which god reveals.

ELECTRA

As you please; I pray the gods. Now, what was in your mind?

OLD MAN

Look now upon this man, my child—your dearest love.

ELECTRA

I have been looking long already; are you crazy?

OLD MAN

And am I crazy if my eyes have seen your brother?

ELECTRA

What have you said, old man? What hopeless impossible
word?

OLD MAN

I said I see Orestes—here—Agamemnon's son.

ELECTRA

How? What sign do you see? What can I know and trust?

OLD MAN

The scar above his eye where once he slipped and drew
blood as he helped you chase a fawn in your father's court.

ELECTRA

I see the mark of a fall, but I cannot believe you.

OLD MAN

How long will you stand, hold back from his arms and love?

ELECTRA

I will not any longer, for my heart has trust
in the token you show.
O Brother so delayed by time,
I hold you against hope . . .

ORESTES

And I hold you at last.

ELECTRA

. . . and never thought I'd see you.

ORESTES

I too abandoned hope.

ELECTRA

And are you he?

ORESTES

I am, your sole defender and friend.
Now if I catch the prey for which I cast my net!°
I'm confident. Or never believe in the gods' power
again if evil can still triumph over good.

CHORUS [*singing*]

You have come, you have come, our slow, bright day,
you have shone, you have shown a beacon-
lit hope for the state, who fled of old
your father's palace, doomed and pained,
drifting in exile.
Now god, some god restores us strong
to triumph, my dear.
Lift high your hands, lift high your voice, raise
prayers to the gods, that in fortune, fortune
your brother may march straight to the city's heart.

ORESTES

Enough. I find sweet pleasure in embrace and welcome,
but let us give ourselves over to pleasure later.
Old man, you came on the crest of opportunity—
tell me what I must do to punish Father's killer
and Mother too who lives in foul adultery.
Have I in Argos any strong measure of friends
or am I bankrupt in backing as I am in fortune?
Whom shall I look to? Shall it be by day or night?
What hunting track will lead me toward my enemies?

OLD MAN

My son, you lost your friends when luck deserted you.
That would indeed be luck met on the road for you,
someone to share both good and evil without change.
But you from root to leaf-top have been robbed of friends
while, leaving, you left them without all hope. Hear me:
in your own hand and in your fortune you hold all,
to capture back your city, home, and patrimony.

ORESTES
But what should we be doing now to reach our goal?

OLD MAN
Kill him. Kill Thyestes' son. And kill your mother.

ORESTES
Such the triumphal crown I came for, yet—how reach it?

OLD MAN
Not inside the city even if you were willing.

ORESTES
Is he so strongly fenced by bodyguards and spears?

OLD MAN
You know it. The man's afraid of you and cannot sleep.

ORESTES
Let that go, then. Tell me another way, old man.

OLD MAN
Yes—you shall hear, for something came to me just now.

ORESTES
I hope your plan and my reaction are equally good.

OLD MAN
I saw Aegisthus as I hauled my way up here.

ORESTES
Good, that sounds hopeful. Where did you happen on him?

OLD MAN
Close, down in the meadows where his horses graze.

ORESTES
What was he doing? Out of despair I see new light.

OLD MAN
Offering a banquet to the goddess nymphs, I think.

ORESTES
To keep his children safe? Or for one not yet born?

OLD MAN
I know only that he was preparing to kill a bull.

ORESTES
How many men were with him? Simply alone with servants?

OLD MAN
No citizens were there; a handful of household servants.

ORESTES
No one who might still recognize my face, old man?

OLD MAN
They are his private servants and they have never seen you.°

ORESTES
And would they, if we conquered, be, ah—kindly disposed?

OLD MAN
That is characteristic of slaves, and luck for you.

ORESTES
How would you suggest my getting close to him?

OLD MAN
Walk past where he will see you as he sacrifices.

ORESTES
He has his fields, I gather, right beside the road?

OLD MAN
And when he sees you he will ask you to join the feast.

ORESTES
He shall find a bitter banquet-fellow, if god wills.

OLD MAN
What happens next—you play it as the dice may fall.

ORESTES
Well spoken. The woman who gave me birth is—where?

OLD MAN
In Argos. She will join him for the feast tonight.

ORESTES
But why did she—my mother—not start out with him?

OLD MAN
The gossip of the crowd disturbs her. She held back.

ORESTES
Of course. She feels the city's disapproving looks.

OLD MAN
That's how it is. Everyone hates a promiscuous wife.

ORESTES
Then how can I kill them both at the same time and place?

ELECTRA
I will be the one to manage my mother's killing.

ORESTES
Good—then fortune will arrange that business well.

ELECTRA
Let our single friend here help the two of us.

OLD MAN
It shall be done. What death have you decided for her?

ELECTRA
Old uncle, you must go to Clytemnestra; tell her°
that I am kept in bed after bearing a son.

OLD MAN
Some time ago? Or has your baby just arrived?

ELECTRA
Ten days ago, which days I have kept ritually clean.

OLD MAN
And how will this achieve the murder of your mother?

ELECTRA
She will come, of course, when she hears about the birth.

OLD MAN

Why? Do you think she cares so deeply for you, child?

ELECTRA

Yes—and she will weep about the boy's low breeding.

OLD MAN

Perhaps. Return now to the goal of your design.

ELECTRA

She will come; she will be killed. All that is clear.

OLD MAN

I see—she comes and walks directly in your door.

ELECTRA

From there she need go only a short way down to Hades.

OLD MAN

I will gladly die too, when I have seen her die.

ELECTRA

But first, old man, you ought to guide Orestes now.

OLD MAN

Where Aegisthus holds his sacrifices to the gods?

ELECTRA

Then go see my mother, tell her all about me.

OLD MAN

I'll speak so well she'll think it is Electra speaking.

ELECTRA *(To Orestes.)*

Your task is ready. You have drawn first chance at killing.

ORESTES

Well, I will go if anyone will show me where.

OLD MAN

I will escort you on your way with greatest joy.

ORESTES°

O Zeus of our Fathers, now be Router of Foes,
have pity on us, for our days are piteous.

OLD MAN

Pity them truly—children sprung of your own blood.

ELECTRA

O Hera, holy mistress of Mycenae's altars,
grant us the victory if our claim to victory is just.

OLD MAN

Grant them at last avenging justice for their father.

ORESTES

And you, O Father, dwelling wronged beneath the earth . . .

ELECTRA

. . . and Earth, ruler below, to whom I stretch my hands . . .

OLD MAN

. . . protect, protect these children here, so dearly loved.

ORESTES

Come now and bring as army all the dead below . . .

ELECTRA

. . . who stood beside you at Troy with the havoc of their spears . . .

OLD MAN

. . . all who hate the godless guilty criminals.

ORESTES

Did you hear us, wretched victim of our mother?°

OLD MAN

All, your father hears all, I know. Time now to march.

ELECTRA

I call to you again and say: "Aegisthus dies!"°
And if, Orestes, in your struggle you should die,

I too am dead, let them no longer say I live,
for I will stab myself with a two-edged sword.
I will go in and make our dwelling fit for the outcome:
then if a message of good fortune comes from you
the whole house shall ring out in triumph. If you die
triumph will shift to desolation. This is my word.

ORESTES

I understand you.

ELECTRA

Make yourself fit man for the hour.
You, my women, with your voices scream a fire-
signal of shouting in this trial. I shall stand guard,
a sword raised ready for the issue in my hand.
If I'm defeated, I shall never grant to those
I hate the right to violate my living flesh.

(Exit Orestes, the Old Man, and Pylades to the side, Electra into the house.)

CHORUS [*singing*]

STROPHE A

The ancient tale is told
in Argos
still—how a magic lamb
from its gentle mother on the hills
Pan stole, Pan of the wild
beasts, kind watcher, Pan
who breathes sweet music to his jointed reed.
He brought it to show the gold
curls of its wool. On the stone
steps a standing herald called:
"To the square, to the square, you men
of Mycenae! Come, run, behold
a strange and lovely thing
for our blessed kings." Swiftly the chorus in dance
beat out honor to Atreus' house.

ANTISTROPHE A

The altars spread their wings
of hammered
gold, fire gleamed in the town
like the moon on Argos' stones
of sacrifice, lotus pipes
tended the Muses, lilting
ripples of tune. The dance swelled in desire
tense for the lamb of gold—
whose? Quick, Thyestes' trick:
seducing in the dark of sleep
Atreus' wife, he brought
the strange lamb home, his own.
Back to the square he calls
all to know how he holds the golden creature,
fleece and horn, in his own house.

STROPHE B

That hour—that hour Zeus
changed the stars on their blazing course,
utterly turned the splendid sun,
turned the white face of the dawn
so the sun drives west over heaven's spine
in glowing god-lit fire.
The watery weight of cloud moved north,
the cracked waste of Egyptian Ammon
dried up, died, never knowing dew,
robbed of the beautiful rain that drops from Zeus.

ANTISTROPHE B

Thus it is always told.
I myself am won only to slight belief
that the sun would swerve or change his gold
countenance of fire, moved in pain
and sorrow at sin in the mortal world,
to judge or punish humans.
Yet terrible myths are useful,

they call men to the worship of the gods—
whom you forgot when you killed your husband,
sister of glorious brothers.

(A cry is heard from offstage.)

Listen, listen.
Friends, did you hear a shout? Or did anxiety
trick me? A shout deep-rolling like the thunder of Zeus?

(Another cry.)

Again it comes! The rising wind is charged with news.
Mistress, come out! Electra, leave the house!

(Enter Electra from the house.)

ELECTRA
Dear friends, what is it? How do we stand now in our trial?

CHORUS
I only know one thing: I heard a voice of death.

ELECTRA
I heard it too. It was far off. But I too heard it.

CHORUS
It comes from a great distance, yet it is quite clear.

ELECTRA
Is it an Argive groaning there—or is it our friends?

CHORUS
I cannot tell; the note of clamoring is slurred.

ELECTRA
So you announce my death by sword. Why am I slow?

CHORUS
Lady, hold back until you learn the outcome clearly.

ELECTRA
Not possible. We are beaten. Where are the messengers?

CHORUS

They will come soon. To kill a king is not quick or light.

(Enter a Messenger, one of Orestes' servants, from the side.)

MESSENGER

Hail maidens of Mycenae, glorious in triumph!
Orestes is victor! I proclaim it to all who love him.
The murderer of Agamemnon lies on the earth
crumpled in blood, Aegisthus. Let us thank the gods.

ELECTRA

Who are you? Why should I think your message is the truth?

MESSENGER

You do not know you're looking on your brother's servant?

ELECTRA

Dearest of servants! Out of fear I held my eyes
shaded from recognition. Now indeed I know you.
What is your news? My father's hated murderer dead?

MESSENGER

Dead, dead. I say it twice if that is what you wish.

ELECTRA

O gods! O Justice watching the world, you have come at last.
How did he die? What style of death did Orestes choose,
to kill Thyestes' son? Give me the details.

MESSENGER

When we rose from your cottage and walked down the hill
we came across a beaten double wagon-track,
and there we found the new commander of Mycenae.
He happened to be walking in the water-meadow,
picking young green shoots of myrtle for his hair.
He saw us and called out: "You are most welcome, strangers.
Who are you? Have you traveled far? Where is your home?"
Orestes answered, "We are Thessalians on our way
toward Alpheus' valley where we shall sacrifice to Zeus

of Olympia." When Aegisthus heard, he called again,
"Now you must stop among us as our guests and share
our feast. I am at the moment slaughtering a bull
for the nymphs. Tomorrow morning you shall rise at dawn
and get there just as soon. Come with me to the house"—
while he was still talking he took us by the hand
and led us off the road—"I will take no refusal."
When we were in the house he gave his men commands:
"Quick, someone fill a bowl of water for the strangers
so their hands will be clean near the lustrations at the altar."
But Orestes interrupted: "We are clean enough.
We washed ourselves just now in the clear river water.
If strangers may join citizens in sacrifice,
we are here, Aegisthus. We shall not refuse you, prince."
So this is what they said in public conversation.
Now the king's bodyguard laid down their spears
and sprang all hands to working.
Some brought the lustral bowl, and others baskets of grain,
some laid and lit the fire or around the hearth
set up the sacred ewers—the whole roof rang with sound.
Your mother's lover took the barley in his hands
and cast it on the altar as he said these words:
"Nymphs of the Rocks, may I kill many bulls for you,
and my wife, Tyndareus' child, who is at home.
Guard us in present fortune, ruin our enemies."
(Meaning you and Orestes.) But my master prayed
the utter reverse, keeping his words below his breath,
to take his dynastic place again. Aegisthus raised
the narrow knife from the basket, cut the calf's front lock,
with his right hand dedicated it to the holy fire,
and, as his servants hoisted the beast upon their shoulders,
slashed its throat.
Now he turns to your brother and says,
"One of your great Thessalian talents, as you boast,
is to be a man of two skills: disjointing bulls

and taming horses. Stranger, take the iron knife,
show us how true Thessalian reputation runs."
Orestes seized the beautifully tempered Dorian blade,
loosened his brooch, flung his fine cloak back from his shoulders,
chose Pylades as his assistant in the work,
and made the men stand off. Holding the calf by its foot,
he laid the white flesh bare by pulling with his hand.
He stripped the hide off whole, more quickly than a runner
racing could double down and back the hippodrome course,
and opened the soft belly. Aegisthus scooped the prophetic
portions up in his hands and looked.
The liver lobe
was missing. But the portal vein and gall sac showed
disaster coming at him even as he looked.
His face darkened, drew down. My master watched and asked,
"What puts you out of heart?" "Stranger, I am afraid.
Some ambush is at my door.° There is a man I hate,
the son of Agamemnon, an enemy to my house."
He answered, "You can scarcely fear a fugitive's
tricks when you control the state? So we can feast
on sacrificial flesh, will someone bring a chopper—
Phthian, not Dorian—and let me split this breastbone?"
He took it and struck. Aegisthus heaped the soft parts, then
sorted them out. But while his head was bent above them,
your brother stretched up, balanced on the balls of his feet,
and smashed a blow to his spine. The vertebrae of his back
broke. Head down, his whole body convulsed, he gasped
to breathe, writhed with a high scream, and died in his blood.
The servingmen who saw it leaped straight to their spears,
an army for two men to face. And yet with courage
they stood, faced them, shook their javelins, engaged—
Pylades and Orestes, who cried, "I have not come
in wrath against this city nor against my servants.

I have only paid my father's killer back in blood.
I am the much-suffering Orestes—do not kill me, men
who helped my father's house of old."
They, when they heard
his words, lowered their spears, and he was recognized
by some old man who used to serve the family.
Swiftly they crowned your brother's head with flower
wreaths,
shouting aloud in joy and triumph. He comes to you
bringing something to show you—not the Gorgon's head,
only Aegisthus whom you loathe, who was in debt
for blood and found the paying bitter at his death.

(Exit to the side.)

CHORUS [*singing*]

STROPHE

Come, lift your foot, lady, to dance
now like a fawn who in flying
arcs leaps for joy, light, almost brushing the sky.
He wins a garland of glory
greater than any Olympic victory,
your own brother; now, in the hymn strain,
praise the fair victor, chant to my step.

ELECTRA

O flame of day and sun's great chariot charged with light,
O earth below and dark of night where I watched before,
my eyes are clear now, I can unfold my sight to freedom,
now that Aegisthus, who had killed my father, falls.
Bring me my few belongings, what my house keeps treasured
as ornaments of splendor for the hair, dear friends,
for I will crown my brother as a conqueror.

CHORUS [*singing*]

ANTISTROPHE

Lay now the bright signs of success
over his brow, as we circle

our chorused step, dancing to the Muses' delight.
Now again in our country
our old and loved kings of the blood capture the power,
in high justice routing the unjust.
Raise to the pipe's tune shouts of our joy.

(Enter Orestes, Pylades, and servants with a corpse from the side.)

ELECTRA

O man of triumph sprung of our triumphant father
who fought and won below the walls of Troy—Orestes!
Take from my hands these woven bindings for your hair.
You come, a runner in no trifling race, but long
and challenging, to your home goal, killing Aegisthus
who was your enemy, who once destroyed our father.
And you, companion of the shield, Pylades, son
of a most pious father, please receive your crown
from my hand, for you have won an equal share of glory
in this trial. May I see your fortune always high!

ORESTES

You must believe, Electra, that the gods have been
first founders of our fortune; then you may turn to praise
me as the simple servant of both god and fortune.
I come to you the killer of Aegisthus, not
in words but action. You know this, but more than this°
I have here in my hands the man himself, quite dead.
You may want to display him for the beasts to eat
or stick him on a stake as a toy for carrion birds
born of bright air. He's yours—once master, now slave.

ELECTRA

I am ashamed to speak and yet I wish to speak.

ORESTES

What is it? Speak your mind, for now you're free from fear.

ELECTRA

I am ashamed to insult the dead; some hate may strike me.

ORESTES

There is no man on earth, nor will be, who could blame you.

ELECTRA

Our city is harsh to please and takes delight in slander.

ORESTES

Speak as you need to, sister. We were joined to him
in bonds of hatred which could know no gentle truce.

ELECTRA

So be it.
Which words of hatred shall I speak in prelude;
which shall I make finale, or marshal in the center?
And yet dawn after dawn I never once have missed
calling aloud what I wished to tell you to your face
if only I were liberated from my fears
now past. We are at that point now. I'll give you the full
torrent of abuse I hoped to tell you living.
You ruined me, orphaned me, and him too, of a father
we loved dearly, though we had done no harm to you.
You bedded my mother in shame, and killed her husband
who captained the Greeks abroad while you skulked far from Phrygia.
You climbed such heights of stupidness that you imagined
your marriage to my mother would not marry you
to cuckoldry, though she had stained our father's bed
adulterously. Know this: when a man seduces another's°
wife in secret sex and then is forced to keep her,
he must be stupid if he thinks that she, unchaste
to her first husband, will suddenly turn chaste for him.
Your household life was painful though you could not see it;
you knew in your heart that you had made a godless marriage,
and Mother knew she had acquired a godless husband,
so each in working evil shouldered the other's load
in mutual pain: she got your evil, you got hers.

Every time you walked outdoors in Argos, you heard
these words: "He's hers." And never: "She belongs to him."
O what perversion, when the woman in the house
stands out as master, not the man. I shake in hate
to see those children whom the city knows and names
not by their father's name but only by their mother's.
It marks the bridegroom who has climbed to a nobler bed;
when no one mentions the husband, everyone knows the wife.
Where you were most deceived in your grand unawareness
was your boast to be a man of power since you had money.
Wealth stays with us a little moment if at all;
only our characters are steadfast, not our possessions,°
for character stays with us to the end and faces
trouble, but unjust wealth dwells with poor fools but then
wings swiftly from their house after brief blossoming.
The women in your life I will not mention—a maiden
ought not—but only hint that I know all about them.
You took liberties since you lived in a grand palace
and were handsome enough. But let me have a husband
not girlish-faced like you but virile and well built,
whose sons would cling bold to the craggy heights of war;
good looks are only ornamental at the dance.
To hell with you! You know not what you did, but time
has found you out. You've paid the price. So should no criminal
who starts his race without a stumble vainly believe
that he has outrun Justice, till in the closing stretch
he nears the finish line and gains life's final goal.

CHORUS LEADER

He wrought horrors, and has paid in horror to you
and your brother. Justice has enormous power.

ELECTRA

Enough now. Servants, take his corpse into the house;

conceal it well in darkness so that when she comes
my mother sees no dead man till her throat is cut.

(The corpse is carried into the house.)

ORESTES°
Hold off a little; let us speak of something else.

ELECTRA
What's there? You see his men from Mycenae coming to help?

ORESTES
Not his men. What I'm seeing is my mother who bore me.

ELECTRA
How beautifully she marches straight into our net!°
See how grandly she rides with chariot and finery.

ORESTES
What—what is our action now toward Mother? Do we kill her?

ELECTRA
Don't tell me pity catches you at the sight of her.

ORESTES
O god!
How can I kill her when she bore me and brought me up?

ELECTRA
Kill her just the way she killed your father and mine.

ORESTES
O Phoebus, your holy word was brute and ignorant . . .

ELECTRA
Where Apollo is ignorant shall men be wise?

ORESTES
. . . that said to kill my mother, whom I must not kill.

ELECTRA

Nothing will hurt you. You are only avenging Father.

ORESTES

As matricide I'll be exiled. But I was clean before.

ELECTRA

Not clean before the gods, if you neglect your father.

ORESTES

I know—but will I not be punished for killing Mother?

ELECTRA

And will you not be punished for not avenging Father?

ORESTES

Did a polluted demon speak in the shape of god?

ELECTRA

Throned on the holy tripod? I shall not believe so.

ORESTES

And I shall not believe those oracles were pure.

ELECTRA

You must not play the coward now and fall to weakness.
Go in. I will bait her a trap as she once baited one°
which sprang at Aegisthus' touch and killed her lawful
husband.

ORESTES

I am going in. I walk a cliff edge in a sea°
of evil, and evil I will do. If the gods approve,
let it be so. This game of death is bitter, not° sweet.

(Exit Orestes and Pylades into the house. Enter Clytemnestra from the side in a chariot, attended by Trojan slaves.)

CHORUS *[chanting]*

Hail! hail!
Queen and mistress of Argos, hail,

Tyndareus' child,
sister in blood to the lordly sons
of Zeus who dwell in starred and flaming
air, saviors adored by men
in the roar of the salt sea.
Hail! I honor you like the gods
for your wealth and brilliant life.
The time to serve° your fortunes
is now, O Queen. Hail!°

CLYTEMNESTRA

Get out of the carriage, Trojan maids; hold my hand
tight, so I can step down safely to the ground.

(They do as instructed.)

Mostly we gave the temples of our gods the spoils
from Phrygia, but these girls, the best in Troy, I chose
to ornament my own house and replace the child
I lost, my loved daughter. The compensation is small.

ELECTRA

Then may not I, who am a slave and also tossed
far from my father's home to live in misery,
may I not, Mother, take your most distinguished hand?

CLYTEMNESTRA

These slaves are here to help me. Do not trouble yourself.

ELECTRA

Why not? You threw me out of home like a war captive;
and with my home destroyed, then I too was destroyed,
as they are too—left dark, lonely, and fatherless.

CLYTEMNESTRA

And dark and lonely were your father's plots against
those he should most have loved and least conspired to kill.
I can tell you—no. When a woman gets an evil
reputation she finds a bitter twist to her words.

This is my case now, but it is not rightly so.
If you have something truly to hate, you ought to learn
the facts first; then hate is more decent. But not in the dark.
My father Tyndareus gave me to your father's care,
not to kill me, not to kill what I bore and loved.
And yet he tempted my daughter, slyly whispering
of marriage with Achilles, took her from home to Aulis
where the ships were stuck, stretched her high above the altar
and, like pale field grass, slashed Iphigenia's throat.
If this had been to save the state from siege and ruin,
if it had helped our home and spared our other children,
to rack one girl for many lives—I could have forgiven.
But now for the sake of Helen's lust and for the man
who took a wife and could not punish her seducer—
for their lives' sake he took the life of my dear child.
I was unfairly wronged in this, yet not for this
would I have gone so savage, nor murdered my own husband,
but he came home to me with a mad, god-filled girl
and introduced her to his bed. So there we were,
two brides being stabled in a single stall.
Oh, women are fools for sex, deny it I shall not.
Since this is in our nature, when our husbands choose
to despise the bed they have, a woman is quite willing
to imitate her man and find another lover.
But then the dirty gossip puts us in the spotlight;
the guilty ones, the men, are never blamed at all.
If Menelaus had been abducted from home on the sly,
should I have had to kill Orestes so my sister's
husband could be rescued? You think your father would
have borne it? Then was it fair for him to kill my child
and not be killed, while he could make me suffer so?
I killed. I turned and walked the only path still open,
straight to his enemies. Would any of his friends
have helped me in the task of murder I had to do?
Speak if you have need or reason. Refute me freely;
demonstrate how your father died without full justice.

CHORUS LEADER

Justice is in your words but your justice is shameful.
A wife should give way to her husband in all things
if her mind is sound; if she refuses to see this truth
she cannot be fully counted in my reckoning.

ELECTRA

Keep in mind, Mother, those last words you spoke,
giving me license to speak out freely against you.

CLYTEMNESTRA

I say them once again, child; I will not deny them.

ELECTRA

But when you hear me, Mother, will you then treat me badly?

CLYTEMNESTRA

Not so at all. I shall be glad to humor you.°

ELECTRA

Then I shall speak—and here is the keynote of my song:
Mother, you who bore me, if only your mind were healthier!
Although for beauty you deserve tremendous praise,
both you and Helen, flowering from a single stalk,
you both grew foolish and have been a disgrace to Castor.
When she was abducted she walked of her own will to ruin,
while you brought ruin on the finest man in Greece
and screened it with the argument that for your child
you killed your husband. The world knows you less well
than I.
You, long before your daughter came near sacrifice,
the very hour your husband marched away from home,
were setting your blond curls by the bronze mirror's light.
Now any woman who works on her beauty when her man
is gone from home indicts herself as being a whore.
She has no decent cause to show her painted face
outside the door unless she wants to look for trouble.
Of all Greek women, you were the only one I know

to hug yourself with pleasure when Troy's fortunes rose,
but when they sank, to cloud your face in sympathy.
You wanted Agamemnon never to come home.
And yet life gave you every chance to be wise and fine.
You had a husband not at all worse than Aegisthus,
whom Greece herself had chosen as her king and captain;
and when your sister Helen did the things she did,
that was your time to capture glory. For black evil
is outlined clearest to our sight by the blaze of virtue.
  Next. If, as you say, our father killed your daughter,
did I do any harm to you, or did my brother?
When you killed your husband, why did you not bestow
the ancestral home on us, but took to bed the gold
which never belonged to you to buy yourself a lover?
And why has he not gone in exile in exchange
for your son's exile, or not have died to pay for me
who still alive have died my sister's death twice over?
If murder judges and calls for murder, I will kill
you—and your son Orestes will kill you—for Father.
If the first death was just, the second too is just.
Whoever has a view to money or to birth°
and marries a bad woman is stupid: better to have
a low-born wife who's chaste than one of noble birth.

CHORUS LEADER

It's luck determines marriage. Some seem to turn out well,
but I have seen that others have been the opposite.

CLYTEMNESTRA

My child, from birth you always have adored your father.
This is part of life. Some children always love
the male; some turn more closely to their mother than to
  him.
I know you and forgive you. I am not so happy
either, child, with what I have done or with myself.
  How poorly you look. Have you not washed? Your clothes
    are bad.°

I suppose you just got up from bed and giving birth?
O god, how miserably my plans have all turned out.
Perhaps I drove my hate too hard against my husband.

ELECTRA
Your mourning comes a little late. There is no cure.
Father is dead now. If you grieve, why not
bring back the son you sent to wander in foreign lands?

CLYTEMNESTRA
I am afraid. I have to watch my life, not his.
They say his father's death has made him very angry.

ELECTRA
Why do you let your husband act like a beast against us?

CLYTEMNESTRA
That is his nature. Yours is wild and stubborn too.

ELECTRA
I was hurt. But I am going to bury my anger soon.

CLYTEMNESTRA
Good; then he never will be harsh to you again.

ELECTRA
He has been haughty; now he is staying in my house.

CLYTEMNESTRA
You see? You want to blow the quarrel to new flames.

ELECTRA
I will be quiet; I fear him—the way I fear him.

CLYTEMNESTRA
Stop this talk. You called me here for something, girl.

ELECTRA
I think that you have heard that I have given birth.
Make me the proper sacrifice—I don't know how—

as the law runs for children at the tenth night moon.
I have no knowledge; I have never had a child.

CLYTEMNESTRA

This is work for the woman who acted as your midwife.

ELECTRA

I acted for myself. I was alone at birth.

CLYTEMNESTRA

Your house is set so desolate of friends and neighbors?

ELECTRA

No one is willing to make friends with poverty.

CLYTEMNESTRA

Then I will go and make the gods full sacrifice
as law prescribes for a child. I give you so much
grace and then pass to the meadow where my husband is,
sacrificing to the nymphs. Servants, take the wagon,
set it in the stables. When you think this rite
of god draws to an end, come back to stand beside me,
for I have debts of grace to pay my husband too.

ELECTRA

Enter our poor house. And, Mother, take good care
the smoky walls put no dark stain upon your robes.
Pay sacrifice to heaven as you ought to pay.

(Exit Clytemnestra into the house, her slaves to the side with the chariot.)

The basket of grain is ready and the knife is sharp
which killed the bull, and close beside him you shall fall
stricken, to keep your bridal rites in the house of death
with him you slept beside in life. I give you so
much grace and you shall give my father grace of justice.

(Exit Electra into the house.)

CHORUS [*singing*]

STROPHE

Evils are interchanging. The winds of this house
shift now to a new track. Of old in the bath
my leader, mine, fell to his death;
the roof rang, the stone heights of the hall echoed loud
to his cry: "O terrible lady, will you kill me now
newly come to my dear land at the tenth cycle of seed?"°

ANTISTROPHE

Justice circles back and brings her to judgment,
she pays grief for love errant. She, when her lord
came safe home, after dragging years,
where his stone Cyclopes' walls rose straight
to the sky, there with steel
freshly honed to an edge killed him, hand on the axe. O wretched
husband, whatever
suffering gripped that cruel woman:
a lioness mountain-bred, ranging out
from her oak-sheltered home, she sprang. It was done.

CLYTEMNESTRA [*singing in this brief lyrical interchange from inside the house while the Chorus sings in reply*]

O children—by the gods—do not kill your mother—no!

CHORUS

Do you hear a cry within the walls?

CLYTEMNESTRA

O, O, I am hurt—

CHORUS

I moan aloud too, to hear her in her children's hands.
Justice is given down by god soon or late;
you suffer terribly now, you acted terribly then,
cruel woman, against your husband.

(*Enter Orestes, Electra, and Pylades from the house, and the corpses of Aegisthus and Clytemnestra are revealed.*)

CHORUS LEADER

Behold them coming from the house in robes of blood
newly stained by a murdered mother, walking straight,°
living signs of triumph over her frightful cries.
There is no house, nor has there been, more suffering
or pitiable than this, the house of Tantalus.

ORESTES [*singing this lyric ode in alternation with Electra and the Chorus*]

STROPHE A

O Earth and Zeus who watch all work
men do, look at this work of blood
and corruption, two bodies in death
lying battered along the dirt°
under my hands, payment
for my pain.

ELECTRA

Weep greatly, my brother, but I am to blame.
A girl burning in hatred I turned against
the mother who bore me.

CHORUS

Weep for destiny; destiny yours°
to mother unforgettable wrath,
to suffer unforgettable pain
beyond pain at your children's hands.
You paid for their father's death as justice asks.

ORESTES

ANTISTROPHE A

Phoebus, you hymned justice in obscure
melody, but the deed has shone
white as a scar. You granted me rest
as murderers rest—to leave the land
of Greece. But where else can I go?
What state, host, god-fearing man

will look steady upon my face,
who killed my mother?

ELECTRA

O weep for me. Where am I now? What dance—
what marriage may I come to? What man will take
me as bride to his bed?

CHORUS

Circling, circling, your uncertain mind
veers in the blowing wind and turns;
you think piously now, but then
thoughtless you did an impious thing,
dear girl, to your brother, whose will was not with you.

ORESTES

STROPHE B

You saw her agony, how she threw aside her dress,
how she was showing her breast there in the midst of death?
My god, how she bent to earth
the limbs which I was born through? and I melted!°

CHORUS

I know, I understand; you have come
through grinding torment hearing her cry
so hurt, your own mother.

ORESTES

ANTISTROPHE B

She broke into a scream then, she stretched up her hand
toward my face: "My son! Oh, be pitiful, my son!"
She clung to my face,
suspended, hanging; my arm dropped with the sword.

CHORUS

Unhappy woman—how could your eyes
bear to watch her blood as your own mother
fought for her breath and died there?

ORESTES

STROPHE C

I snatched a fold of my cloak to hood my eyes, and, blind,
took the sword and sacrificed
my mother—sank steel into her neck.

ELECTRA

I urged you on, I urged you on,
I touched the sword beside your hand,
I worked a terrible pain and ruin.°

ORESTES°

ANTISTROPHE C

Take it! shroud my mother's dead flesh in a cloak;
clean and close the sucking wounds.
Your own murderers were the children you bore.

ELECTRA

Behold! I wrap her close in this robe,
her whom I loved and could not love,
ending our family's great disasters.

(Enter the Dioscuri above the house.)

CHORUS [*now chanting*]

Whom do I see high over your house
shining in radiance? Are they hero spirits
or gods of the heavens? They are more than men
in their moving. Why do they come so bright
into the eyes of mortals?

CASTOR [*speaking for both Dioscuri*]

O son of Agamemnon, hear us: we call to you,
the Twins, born with your mother, named the sons of Zeus,
I Castor, and my brother Polydeuces here.
We come to Argos having turned the rolling storm
of a sea-tossed ship to quiet, when we saw the death
of this our murdered sister, your murdered mother.

Justice has claimed her, but you have not worked in justice.
As for Phoebus, Phoebus—yet he is my lord,
silence. He knows what is wise, but his oracles were not wise.
Compulsion is on us all to accept this, and in future
to go complete those things which fate and Zeus assigned you.
   Give Pylades Electra as a wife in his house,
and leave Argos yourself. The city is not yours
to walk in any longer, since you killed your mother.
The dreadful beast-faced goddesses of destiny
will roll you like a wheel through maddened wandering.
But when you come to Athens, fold the holy wood
of Pallas' statue to your breast—then she will check
the fluttering horror of their snakes, they cannot touch you
as she holds her Gorgon-circled shield above your head.
In Athens is the Hill of Ares, where the gods
first took their seats to judge murder by public vote,
the time raw-minded Ares killed Halirrhothius
in anger at his daughter's godless wedding night,
in anger at the sea lord's son. Since then this court
has been holy and trusted by both men and gods.
There you too must run the risk of trial for murder.
But the voting pebbles will be cast equal and save you;
you shall not die by the verdict: Loxias will take
all blame on himself for having required your mother's
   death,
and so for the rest of time this law shall be established:
"When votes are equal the accused must have acquittal."
The dreadful goddesses, shaken in grief for this,
shall go down in a crack of earth beside the Hill
to keep a dark and august oracle for men.
Then you must found a city near Arcadian
Alpheus' stream, beside the wolf god's sanctuary.
and by your name that city shall be known to men.
   So much I say to you. Aegisthus' corpse the men
of Argos will hide, buried in an earth-heaped tomb.

Menelaus will bury your mother. He has come just now
to Nauplia for the first time since he captured Troy.
Helen will help him. She is home from Proteus' halls,
leaving Egypt behind. She never went to Troy.
Instead, Zeus made and sent a Helen-image there
to Ilium so men might die in hate and blood.
So. Let Pylades take Electra, girl and wife,
and start his journey homeward, leaving Achaea's lands;
let him also to his Phocian estates escort
her "husband," as they call him—set him deep in wealth.
Turn your feet toward Isthmus' narrow neck of earth;
make your way to the blessed hill where Cecrops dwelt.
When you have drained the fullness of this murder's doom
you will again be happy, released from these distresses.

CHORUS [*chanting from now until the end of the play, like all the other characters*]

Sons of Zeus, does the law allow us
to draw any closer toward your voice?

CASTOR

The law allows; you are clean of this blood.

ELECTRA

Will you speak to me too, Tyndarids?°

CASTOR

Also to you. On Phoebus I place all
guilt for this death.

CHORUS

Why could you, who are gods and brothers
of the dead woman here,
not turn her Furies away from our halls?

CASTOR

Fate is compelling; it leads and we follow—
fate and the unwise song of Apollo.

ELECTRA

And I? What Apollo, what oracle's voice
ordained I be marked in my mother's blood?

CASTOR

You shared in the act, you share in the fate:
both children a single
curse on your house has ground into dust.

ORESTES

O sister, I found you so late, and so soon
I lose you, robbed of your healing love,
and leave you behind as you leave me.

CASTOR

She has a husband, she has a home, she
needs no pity, she suffers nothing
but exile from Argos.

ELECTRA

Are there more poignant sorrows or greater
than leaving the soil of a fatherland?

ORESTES

But I go too; I am forced from my father's
home; I must suffer foreigners' judgment
for the blood of my mother.

CASTOR

Courage. You go
to the holy city of Pallas. Endure.

ELECTRA

Hold me now closely breast against breast,
dear brother. I love you.
But the curses bred in a mother's blood
dissolve our bonds and drive us from home.

ORESTES

Come to me, clasp my body, lament
as if at the tomb of a man now dead.

CASTOR

Alas, your despair rings terribly, even
to listening gods;
pity at mortal labor and pain still
lives in us and the lords of heaven.

ORESTES

I shall not see you again.

ELECTRA

I shall never more walk in the light of your eye.

ORESTES

Now is the last I can hear your voice.

ELECTRA

Farewell, my city.
Many times farewell, women of my city.

ORESTES

O loyal love, do you go so soon?

ELECTRA

I go. These tears are harsh for my eyes.

ORESTES

Pylades, go, farewell; and be kind to
Electra in marriage.

CASTOR

Marriage shall be their care. But the hounds
are here. Quick, to Athens! Run to escape,
for they hurl their ghostly tracking against you,
serpent-fisted and blackened of flesh,
offering the fruit of terrible pain.

We two must hurry to Sicilian seas,
rescue the salt-smashed prows of the fleet.
As we move through the open valleys of air
we champion none who are stained in sin,
but those who have held the holy and just
dear in their lives we will loose from harsh
toils and save them.
So let no man be desirous of evil
nor sail with those who have broken their oaths—
as god to men I command you.

(Exit with Polydeuces.)

CHORUS

Farewell. The mortal who can fare well,°
not broken by trouble met on the road,
leads a most blessed life.

(Exit all.)

TEXTUAL NOTES

(Line numbers are in some cases only approximate.)

ANDROMACHE

6: This verse is followed in the medieval manuscripts by one line (7): "was born than I am or will ever be." This line is omitted by the only ancient papyrus that transmits this part of the play and is said in the ancient commentaries to have been inserted into the text by actors; it is rejected by almost all modern scholars as an interpolation.

70: This line is transmitted in the manuscripts after line 72 and is transposed to this place after line 69 by some modern scholars.

154: This line is rejected by many scholars as an interpolation.

195: Text uncertain.

273: This line is rejected by some scholars as an interpolation.

321–23: These lines are rejected by many scholars as an interpolation.

330–33: These lines are rejected by most scholars as an interpolation.

365: A line may be missing before this verse.

397–98: These lines are rejected by many scholars as an interpolation.

668–77: These lines are rejected by some scholars as an interpolation.

699–702: These lines are rejected by some scholars as an interpolation.

743: This line is rejected by some scholars as an interpolation.

810: This line is rejected by many scholars as an interpolation.

878: This line is rejected by most scholars as an interpolation.

929: The manuscripts transmit this line with "how did you . . . go wrong" instead of "how did I . . . go wrong" and hence attribute the line to Orestes; the translation reflects a modern emendation accepted by many scholars.

937: This line is rejected by most scholars as an interpolation.

962: Instead of "murder," which is transmitted by only one manuscript of the play but is accepted by many modern scholars, most of the medieval manuscripts read "fear," and one ancient papyrus reads "jealousy."

964: Text uncertain.

1031–35: Text uncertain.

1038–39: Text uncertain.

1047: Text uncertain.

1151: This line is rejected by many scholars as an interpolation.

1171–72: Text uncertain.

1189–92: Text uncertain.

1205: This verse is followed in the manuscripts by one line (1206): "Oh, poor me, unhappy me." There is no corresponding line in the antistrophe at this point, so either one line has been lost there (after 1219) or this line should be deleted as an interpolation. Most scholars prefer the latter.

[1254]: According to ancient commentaries, line 1254 was missing in many ancient manuscripts of the play; it is transferred to between lines 1235 and 1236 by most modern scholars.

1279–82: These lines are rejected by some scholars as an interpolation.

1283: This line is quoted by an ancient author who attributes it not to this play but to Euripides' lost *Antiope*; it is rejected here by many scholars as an interpolation.

1284–88: These lines are rejected by some scholars as an interpolation.

HECUBA

74–76: These lines are rejected as interpolations by many scholars; the text of the last one is uncertain.

90–97: Some or all of these lines are rejected as interpolations by many scholars.

145: This line is rejected as an interpolation by some scholars.

175–76: These lines are rejected as interpolations by many scholars.

206: Some words seem to be missing after this line.

211–15: These lines are rejected as interpolations by some scholars.

415–20: Different scholars have proposed various rearrangements of these lines.

555–56: These lines are rejected as interpolations by many scholars.

599–602: These lines are rejected as interpolations by many scholars.

793–97: These lines are rejected as interpolations by most scholars.

830: After this line the manuscripts transmit two lines, "From darkness and the delights of night comes the greatest pleasure for mortals" (831–32); these are rejected as interpolations by most scholars.

847: Text uncertain.

859: The manuscripts read "to you"; the translation reflects a widely accepted modern scholarly emendation.

953: This line is rejected as an interpolation by many scholars.

973–75: These lines are rejected as an interpolation by many scholars.

1041: Some manuscripts assign this line to Polymestor, some to the Chorus Leader, some to a half chorus; most modern scholars give it to Polymestor.

1086: After this line the manuscripts transmit a line: "Some divinity has given this who is heavy upon you" (1087); it is almost identical with line 723 and is rejected as an interpolation here by most scholars.

1184: After this line the manuscripts transmit two lines, "For there are many of us: some are odious, others have been born into the ranks of the evil " (1185–86); these are rejected as interpolations by most scholars.

THE SUPPLIANT WOMEN

44–45: Text uncertain.

72: It is uncertain who exactly is meant: the temple servants (cf. line 2) or, likelier, servants of the mothers of the Seven.

162: This line is deleted by some scholars as an interpolation and is assigned to Theseus by others.

179: Some lines seem to have been lost after this line.

221: The manuscript reads “the gods live”; the translation reflects a widely accepted scholarly emendation.

249: Text uncertain.

252: This sentence is deleted by many scholars as an interpolation.

263–70: These lines are assigned by the manuscript to Adrastus; many scholars give them instead to the Chorus Leader. In any case some lines seem to be missing before line 263.

271–85: Some scholars assign different parts of this song to different sections of the chorus.

275–76: The text of these lines is uncertain; they are deleted by many scholars as an interpolation.

280: Text uncertain.

303: Text uncertain; this sentence is deleted by many scholars as an interpolation.

435–36: These lines are deleted by some scholars as an interpolation.

598–633: This choral ode is assigned by the manuscript to Aethra and the chorus in alternation; scholars assign it instead to two half choruses or to individual members of the chorus in alternation. A dash signals a change of singer.

599: Text uncertain.

763: A line with Adrastus’ question is missing after this verse; the translation gives its probable sense.

805: Most of a line with Adrastus’ lament and the chorus’ response is missing after this verse.

838: Text uncertain.

843: After this verse, two lines are transmitted (844–45) which are clearly out of place here and are transposed by scholars to follow line 859.

844–45: See on line 843.

900: Text uncertain.

907: Four lines (902–6) follow: “He was not illustrious in words but was a formidable expert with his shield and smart at inventing many things. Though his brother Meleager was more intelligent than he was, he achieved equal renown by the art of the spear, inventing exact music on the shield." Most scholars reject all or some of these lines as interpolated.

990–1008, 1012–30: The text of Evadne's song is very uncertain.

1012–30: See previous note.

1092–93: These lines are deleted by some scholars as an interpolation.

1122–64: Scholars disagree about just which lines in this choral duet between the chorus of old women and the chorus of boys are to be assigned to each of the two groups of singers.

1142–44: Text uncertain.

ELECTRA

1: Text uncertain.

131: The manuscript reads "are you a slave"; the translation reflects a plausible modern emendation.

143–44: The text of these lines is corrupt, but their meaning is clear.

161–62: The text of these lines is very uncertain.

277: The text is corrupt but the general meaning is clear.

311: Text and meaning uncertain.

373–79: These lines are rejected by many scholars as an interpolation.

386–90: These lines are rejected by many scholars as an interpolation.

413: This phrase seems corrupt but its general sense is not in doubt.

460: Text and meaning uncertain.

484: The manuscript is corrupt here; the translation reflects a plausible modern emendation.

538: Many scholars suggest that a line has been lost in the text after this verse.

546: Text uncertain, and many scholars suggest that another line is missing after this one.

582: A line has probably been lost after this verse.

631: The manuscript reads "and I have never seen them"; the translation reflects a plausible modern emendation.

651–52: Some scholars suggest that line 651 should be rejected as an interpolation, while others suggest that it be kept but that another line has been lost in the text after it.

671–84: The assignment of verses to the individual speakers in this passage is uncertain.

682–92: The sequence, authenticity, and meaning of these lines are very uncertain.

685–89: Many scholars reject these lines as an interpolation.

832: Or "some ambush comes from abroad."

894: The text and meaning of these words are uncertain.

921–37: Some scholars suspect some of these lines of being interpolated.

941–44: Some scholars suspect these lines of being interpolated.

962–65: The manuscript assigns line 962 to Electra, 963 to Orestes, 964 to Electra, and 965 to Orestes; the translation reflects the consensus of modern scholars.

965: Many scholars suggest that a line spoken by Orestes has been lost in the text after this verse.

983–84: Text very uncertain.

985–86: Some editors emend to "I am beginning to step forward, and evil I will do."

987: The Greek manuscript reads "bitter and sweet"; the translation reflects a widely accepted modern scholarly emendation.

996: The Greek verb can mean "serve, worship, flatter, cure medically"; all these meanings are pertinent here.

997: The last words of the chorus' anapests here are corrupt.

1059: The text is uncertain but its meaning is clear.

1097–1101: These lines are rejected by most scholars as an interpolation.

1107–8: Some scholars transpose these two lines to follow line 1131.

1153: After these words, the last two lines of this strophe are missing in the manuscript.

1173: Many scholars suggest that a line has been lost in the text after this verse.

1180–82: The first of these lines is corrupt and a couple of lines have been lost after it.

1185–86: The text of these lines is uncertain.

1209: The manuscript reads "and her hair!"; the translation reflects a widely accepted modern scholarly emendation.

1226: This line is assigned to the chorus in the manuscript, but most modern scholars give it instead to Electra.

1227–29: These lines are assigned to the chorus in the manuscript, but most modern scholars give them instead to Orestes.

1295–97: Some scholars transpose these lines to follow line 1302.

1357–59: Some scholars reject these lines as an interpolation.

GLOSSARY

Achaea, Achaeans: a region (and its people) in Greece on the northern coast of the Peloponnese; sometimes used to refer to all of Greece (and its people).

Achelous: an important river in western Greece.

Achilles: son of Peleus and father of Neoptolemus; the greatest warrior of the Greeks at Troy.

Adrastus: king of Argos; leader of the Seven against Thebes.

Aeacus: legendary king of Aegina; father of Peleus.

Aegeus: legendary hero of Athens; father of Theseus.

Aegialeus: son of Adrastus.

Aegisthus: son of Thyestes; cousin of Agamemnon; lover of Clytemnestra, he killed Agamemnon with her and was killed by Orestes.

Aegyptus: in Greek mythology, a legendary king of Egypt, forty-nine of whose fifty sons were murdered by the fifty daughters of his brother Danaus.

Aethra: legendary heroine of Athens; daughter of Pittheus and mother of Theseus.

Aetolia: a mountainous area of central Greece on the northern coast of the Gulf of Corinth.

Agamemnon: son of Atreus; leader of the Greek army at Troy; brother of Menelaus; husband of Clytemnestra, killed by her and Aegisthus upon his return from Troy; father of Iphigenia, Electra, and Orestes.

Alpheus: a river in the Peloponnese in southern Greece; it flows along Olympia, the site of an important Greek religious center.

Ammon: an important Egyptian god, worshipped there and in neighboring countries at various temples with which oracles were associated.

Amphiaraus: seer and king of Argos; brother-in-law of Adrastus; the most positively portrayed of the Seven against Thebes, he was not killed but swallowed up alive by the earth together with his chariot.

Amphion: one of the two mythic builders of Thebes, together with his twin brother Zethus; his tomb was located to the north of Thebes.

Andromache: during the Trojan War, the wife of Hector and mother of Astyanax; afterward, the concubine of Neoptolemus and mother of a child with him; later, the wife of Helenus.

Aphrodite: goddess of sexual desire.

Apidanus: a river in Thessaly.

Apollo: son of Zeus and Leto; twin brother of Artemis; god of prophecy, healing, and poetry; his prophetic seat was at Delphi.

Arcadia, Arcadians: a region (and its people) in southern Greece in the central and eastern part of the Peloponnese.

Ares: god of war.

Argives: the inhabitants of Argos; in general, all the Greeks.

Argo: the boat on which Jason and his crew, the Argonauts (including Peleus), sailed on their quest to obtain the Golden Fleece.

Argos: a city and region in the eastern Peloponnnese in southern Greece, not always distinguished clearly from Mycenae.

Artemis: daughter of Zeus and Leto; twin sister of Apollo; goddess of the hunt, childbirth, and virginity, who protected wild animals and boys and girls before they reached adolescence; sometimes identified with Hecate.

Asopus: a river in Boeotia that flows near Thebes.

Astyanax: son of Hector and Andromache; hurled from the walls of Troy when the Greeks sacked the city.

Atalanta: a legendary huntress; mother of Parthenopaeus (one of the Seven against Thebes).

Athena: daughter of Zeus and Metis; goddess of wisdom, warfare, and weaving; patron goddess of Athens.

Athens: city of southeastern Greece, named after Athena and protected by her.

Atreus: father of Agamemnon and Menelaus; brother of Thyestes.

Aulis: a harbor in eastern Greece in Boeotia, from which the Greek fleet set sail for Troy; when they were held back by adverse weather, Agamemnon was thought to have sacrificed his daughter Iphigenia to Artemis there.

Bacchants: ecstatic female worshippers of Dionysus.

Cadmus: originally a Phoenician prince, founder of the Greek city of Thebes.

Capaneus: husband of Evadne; one of the most negatively portrayed of the Seven against Thebes; he boasted that he would sack the city whether Zeus wished it or not, and while he was mounting a ladder to attack the city Zeus killed him with a thunderbolt.

Cassandra: prophetic daughter of Priam and Hecuba; she is brought home by Agamemnon as his concubine and is murdered by Clytemnestra there.

Castor: together with Polydeuces (or Pollux), one of the twin sons of Tyndareus; brother of Helen and Clytemnestra; a divinity who protected mariners in distress.

Cecropia: an archaic name for the acropolis of Athens, from the legendary King Cecrops of Athens.

Centaurs: mythical figures, half horse, half human; when they got drunk and became violent at the wedding of Pirithous, they fought with the Lapiths and were killed by them.

Chersonese: a peninsula across the Hellespont from Troy; called the Thracian Chersonese to distinguish it from the Grecian Chersonese in the northern part of Greece.

Cisseus: a legendary Thracian king, according to some accounts the father of Hecuba.

Cithaeron: a mountain in central Greece near Thebes.

Clashing Rocks: the two rocks (Symplegades), located at either side of the Bosphorus, that were said to crash together at random and crush ships as they passed through.

Clytemnestra: wife of Agamemnon, who together with her lover Aegisthus killed him on his return from Troy; mother of Iphigenia, Electra, and Orestes, who killed her in revenge for his father's death. Also written Clytaemestra.

Cranaid: descendant of Cranaus, a legendary king of Athens; in general, any Athenian.

Creon: king of Thebes after the destitution of Oedipus and the deaths of Eteocles and Polynices.

Cyclopes: mythical builders of the walls of Mycenae and other cities.

Cypris: Aphrodite, who was born in the sea near the island of Cyprus.

Danaans: descendants of Danaus; in general, Argives and, more generally, all the Greeks.

Danaus: a hero who was one of the legendary founders of Argos.

Dardanus: a hero who was one of the legendary founders of Troy.

Delos: a Greek island, birthplace of Apollo and Artemis and a center of their worship.

Delphi: the major oracle and cult center of Apollo, situated on Mount Parnassus in central Greece.

Demeter: goddess of fertility, mother of Persephone.

Diomedes: son of Tydeus (one of the Seven against Thebes); he attacked and defeated Thebes in the following generation and was an important Greek warrior in the Trojan War.

Dionysus: son of Zeus and Semele, associated with Thrace; god of wine and theater.

Dioscuri: Castor and Polydeuces (Pollux), the twin brothers of Helen and Clytemnestra; divinities who protected mariners in distress.

Dirce: a fountain in Thebes.

Dodona: an oracle of Zeus in Epirus in northwestern Greece.

Dorian: belonging to one of the four major tribes of ancient Greece, especially associated with Sparta and the Peloponnese.

Doris: a region in central Greece, traditionally the homeland of the Dorians.

Electra: daughter of Agamemnon and Clytemnestra; sister of Iphigenia and Orestes.

Electra gate: one of the city gates of Thebes, leading out toward Cithaeron.

Eleusis: a town in Attica to the northwest of Athens; an important religious center, site of the Eleusinian Mysteries of Demeter and Persephone.

Eleutherae: a town in the northern part of Attica near its border with Boeotia.

Epidaurian weapon: the bronze club with which the brigand Periphetes killed travelers; after Theseus killed him, he took and used the weapon himself.

Erechtheus: a legendary king of Athens.

Eteocles: son of Oedipus; brother of Polynices, Antigone, and Ismene.

Eteoclus: one of the Seven against Thebes.

Euboea: a large island off the coast of eastern mainland Greece, north of Athens.

Eurotas: a river near Sparta in the Peloponnese.

Evadne: wife of Capaneus.

Fount of the Dance: Callichorus, a sacred spring at Eleusis.

Furies: monstrous female divinities of vengeance, who punished especially murder within the family.

Gorgon: one of three monstrous snake-women killed by Perseus; their terrifying hideousness turned onlookers to stone.

Hades: brother of Zeus and Poseidon; god of the underworld; his name is used synonymously for the underworld itself.

Halirrhothius: a son of Poseidon who raped Ares' daughter Alcippe; Ares killed him in revenge and was tried, and acquitted, in the first court of law, on the Areopagus ("Hill of Ares") in Athens near the Acropolis.

Hector: son of Priam and Hecuba; husband of Andromache; the greatest warrior of the Trojans against the Greeks; he was killed by Achilles.

Hecuba: queen of Troy, wife of Priam, and, according to some acounts, mother of fifty sons and daughters.

Helen: wife of Menelaus (the brother of Agamemnon) and mother of Hermione; her elopement with Paris caused the Trojan War.

Helenus: a son of Priam; a Trojan seer; after the defeat of Troy he married Andromache and founded a dynasty of rulers in Epirus.

Hellas: Greece.

Hephaestus: the divine smith and craftsman of the gods; he made a splendid new suit of armor for Achilles.

Hera: wife and sister of Zeus; queen of the gods; goddess of marriage; she had an important cult center at Argos.

Heracles: son of Zeus and Alcmene; the greatest hero of Greek legend, famous for his physical strength and for his wildness in drinking and sexuality; he led a first Greek expedition that conquered Troy in the generations before the Trojan War celebrated by Homer.

Hermes: son of Zeus and Maia; the messenger god; god of travelers, contests, stealth, and heralds, who accompanied the souls of the dead to the underworld.

Hermione: daughter of Menelaus and Helen.

Hill of Ares: the Areopagus, a hill in Athens near the Acropolis, site of an important court of law.

Hippomedon: one of the Seven against Thebes.

Hyades: nymphs, daughters of Atlas, sisters of the Pleiades, who like them were turned into a cluster of stars.

Ida: a mountain near Troy, where Paris judged a beauty contest between Hera, Athena, and Aphrodite; Paris assigned the victory to Aphrodite, who rewarded him with Helen.

Ilium: Troy.

Inachus: the main river of Argos; father of Io, who bore to Zeus the founder of the royal house of Argos; Io was transformed into a heifer.

Iphigenia: daughter of Agamemnon and Clytemnestra; when adverse winds blocked the Greek fleet at Aulis from sailing to Troy, Agamemnon had her brought to Aulis and was thought to have sacrificed her to Artemis there (in fact, Artemis spirited her away to the land of the Taurians and put a deer in her place).

Iphis: father of Eteoclus (one of the Seven against Thebes) and of Evadne, wife of Capaneus (another of the Seven).

Ismenian hill: a hill to the southeast of Thebes.

Ismenus: a river in Boeotia that flows through Thebes.

Isthmus: the narrow strip of land connecting the Peloponnese in southern Greece to the rest of mainland Greece.

Laconia: a region in southern Greece in the southeastern part of the Peloponnese; Sparta is situated there.

Lapiths: a legendary people of Thessaly who fought with the Centaurs at the wedding of Pirithous and killed them.

Lemnos: an island in the northern part of the Aegean Sea; according to legend, its female inhabitants went mad and killed all their male relatives.

Leto: goddess, the mother of Apollo and Artemis.

Leuke: an island in the Black Sea to which according to some versions Achilles was transported after his death.

Loxias: Apollo; the word means "slanting" and may refer to the ambiguity of his oracles.

Maia: a nymph, who bore Hermes to Zeus.

Menelaus: brother of Agamemnon; husband of Helen; father of Hermione.

Molossia: a region in Epirus in western Greece.

Muses: daughters of Mnemosyne and Zeus, associated with all forms of cultural, especially artistic, excellence.

Mycenae, Mycenaeans: an ancient city (and its people) in the northeastern Peloponnese in southern Greece, not always distinguished clearly from Argos.

Nauplia: a harbor on the eastern coast of the Peloponnese.

Neoptolemus: son of Achilles, notorious for his brutality at the sack of Troy (he killed Priam at an altar); afterward he took Andromache as slave and concubine, and was killed at Delphi; also known as Pyrrhus.

Nereid: one of the fifty sea nymphs, daughters of Nereus.

Nereus: a divinity of the sea, father of the fifty Nereids.

Nile: the most important river of Egypt, one of the largest rivers known to the ancient world.

Nymphs: female divinities who protected the young.

Odysseus: Greek warrior at Troy, famous for his cleverness.

Oecles: father of Amphiaraus.

Oedipus: legendary ruler of Thebes; son of Laius and Jocasta; husband of Jocasta; father and brother of Eteocles, Polynices, Antigone, and Ismene.

Olympia: an important cult center of Zeus in the region of Elis in the western Peloponnese, site of the most important Greek athletic festival, held every four years.

Olympic: referring to the athletic festival in Olympia.

Orestes: son of Agamemnon and Clytemnestra; brother of Iphigenia and Electra; he killed his mother to avenge his father.

Orion: a legendary monstrous hunter, placed after his death among the stars.

Ossa: a mountain in the region of Thessaly in north-central Greece; when the Giants Otus and Ephialtes attempted to storm Olympus, they piled Ossa on Pelion.

Pallas: Athena.

Pan: a rustic, musical god dwelling in wild nature and associated with sudden mental disturbances (hence our term "panic").

Pandion: a legendary king of Athens.

Paris: son of Priam and Hecuba; his elopement with Helen caused the Trojan War.

Parnassus: a mountain above Delphi in central Greece.

Parthenopaeus: one of the Seven against Thebes.

Peirene: a nymph whose son with Poseidon, Cenchrias, was accidentally killed by Artemis; she became a spring outside Corinth.

Peleus: father of Achilles.

Pelion: a mountain in the southeastern part of Thessaly in north-central Greece; when the Giants Otus and Ephialtes attempted to storm Olympus, they piled Ossa on Pelion.

Pelops: a king of the city of Pisa in the Peloponnese in southern Greece; father of Pittheus.

Pelops' land: the Peloponnese in southern Greece.

Persephone: daughter of Demeter; queen of the underworld.

Perseus: legendary hero who killed the Gorgon Medusa.

Pharsala: a town in southern Thessaly in north-central Greece.

Phasis: a Greek colony on the eastern coast of the Black Sea.

Phocis, Phocian: a region (and its people) in central Greece on the northern shore of the Gulf of Corinth.

Phocus: son of Aeacus; brother of Peleus and Telamon, who killed him and then fled from Aegina.

Phoebus: epithet of Apollo meaning "bright."

Phorbas: a legendary Athenian hero associated with Theseus.

Phrygia, Phrygian: a kingdom (and its people) in what is now west-central Turkey; often used as a synonym for Troy (and its people).

Phthia, Phthian: a region (and its people) in southern Thessaly in north-central Greece.

Pittheus: a king of Troezen; son of Pelops; grandfather of Theseus; regarded as one of the wise men of antiquity.

Pleiades: nymphs, daughters of Atlas, sisters of the Hyades, who like them were turned into a cluster of stars.

Polydeuces: together with Castor, one of the twin sons of Tyndareus; brother of Helen and Clytemnestra; a divinity who protected mariners in distress; also known as Pollux.

Polydorus: youngest son of Priam and Hecuba.

Polymestor: king of Thrace.

Polynices: son of Oedipus; brother of Eteocles, Antigone, and Ismene.

Polyxena: daughter of Priam and Hecuba; sacrificed to the dead Achilles after the fall of Troy.

Priam: king of Troy; husband of Hecuba.

Proteus: originally a sea god, identified with a mythical Egyptian king celebrated for his wisdom; according to some versions, the real Helen stayed with him while an image of her was brought to Troy by Paris and was fought over during the Trojan War; after the war, Menelaus found her in Egypt and brought her home.

Pylades: son of Strophius of Phocis; the loyal and mostly silent comrade of Orestes.

Pyrrhic: a kind of war dance said to have been invented by Neoptolemus (who was also known as Pyrrhus).

Pythian: Delphic.

Pytho: another name for Delphi, from the dragon that Apollo slew when he came to found his cult there.

Scyros: an island of the Sporades group in the Aegean Sea; Neoptolemus came from there, and Theseus was said to have been buried there.

Scythians: a nomadic barbarian people living to the north and east of the Black Sea.

Sea god: Poseidon.

Sepias: a promontory on the coast of Thessaly in east-central Greece.

Seven against Thebes: the six champions who aided Polynices (the seventh one) in his failed attempt to attack seven-gated Thebes with an army from Argos and regain the power and wealth which Polynices' brother had denied him; the names of the seven champions in Euripides' play are Amphiaraus, Capaneus, Eteoclus, Hippomedon, Parthenopaeus, Polynices, and Tydeus.

Sicilian: of Sicily, an island to the southwest of Italy; during the Peloponnesian War the Athenians attacked the island and were disastrously defeated.

Simois: a river near Troy.

Sirens: mythical female singers whose song was fatally seductive.

Sirius: the brightest star in the night sky.

Sown Man: according to Theban legend, the original inhabitants of the city sprang from the ground, from the teeth of a dragon that Cadmus sowed.

Sparta: a city in the southeastern Peloponnese in southern Greece.

Sphinxes: monstrous deadly mythical figures, part woman, part animal.

Spring of Ares: a fountain to the southwest of Thebes.

Strophius: king of Phocis; father of Pylades; when Clytemnestra and Aegisthus killed Agamemnon, Orestes was rescued and brought to Strophius for safekeeping.

Talthybius: a herald of the Greek army at Troy.

Tanaus: a small river near Argos in the eastern Peloponnnese in southern Greece.

Tantalus: father of Pelops; founder of the house of Atreus to which Agamemnon and Aegisthus belonged.

Thebe: a town in Mysia in northwest Anatolia (now northwestern Turkey) from which Andromache came.

Thebes: a city in the southern part of the region of Boeotia in central Greece.

Theseus: son of Aegeus and Aethra; the most important hero of Athenian legend.

Thessaly, Thessalians: a large region (and its people) in the north-central part of Greece.

Thetideion: a small town with a temple to Thetis in Thessaly in the north-central part of Greece.

Thetis: sea nymph, one of the fifty daughters of Nereus; wife of Peleus and mother of Achilles.

Thrace: a region on the coast of the northeastern Aegean Sea inhabited by wild barbarians.

Thyestes: brother of Atreus, bound to him by a furious hatred; father of Aegisthus.

Titans: primeval divinities, defeated by Zeus, Athena, and the other Olympian gods.

Troy: city in northwestern Anatolia (now northwestern Turkey), defeated and pillaged by a Greek army.

Tydeus: one of the Seven against Thebes; father of Diomedes.

Tyndareus: husband of Leda; father of Castor and Polydeuces, and of Helen and Clytemnestra.

Tyndarids: children of Tyndareus.

War god: Ares.

Zeus: father of the Olympian gods; king of gods and men.

Made in the USA
Coppell, TX
08 September 2024

36961466R00154